In the Twinkling of an Eye

In the Twinkling of an Eye

Transforming the Heart One Miracle at a Time

by Paul Cummings

Foreword by Ian Heard

RESOURCE *Publications* · Eugene, Oregon

IN THE TWINKLING OF AN EYE
Transforming the Heart One Miracle at a Time

Resource Publications
An Imprint of Wipf and Stock Publishers
199 W. 8th Ave., Suite 3
Eugene, OR 97401

www.wipfandstock.com

PAPERBACK ISBN: 978-1-5326-9407-3
HARDCOVER ISBN: 978-1-5326-9408-0
EBOOK ISBN: 978-1-5326-9409-7

Manufactured in the U.S.A.   AUGUST 15, 2019

To all those who didn't give up on me.
Especially my beautiful Chris.

The veils of the future are lifted one by one,
and mortals must act from day to day.

SIR WINSTON S. CHURCHILL, *THE GATHERING STORM*

Contents

Foreword by Ian Heard / ix

Preface / xi

Acknowledgments / xiii

Introduction / xv

Chapter 1   Beginnings / 1

Chapter 2   Poorboy Club / 5

Chapter 3   Jesus Lovers or Jesus Cult? / 15

Chapter 4   Australian Pain and God's Hope / 21

Chapter 5   All, or Nothing . . . / 28

Chapter 6   A Few Steps from the Brink / 32

Chapter 7   Devil's Darkness to Light in Jesus / 36

Chapter 8   Jehovah's Witnesses / 41

Chapter 9   Potty Mouth / 46

Chapter 10   Father God / 51

Chapter 11   Audio Visual / 60

Chapter 12   You Don't Smoke Anymore / 66

Chapter 13   Getting a Wife / 71

Chapter 14   Opening Windows / 75

Chapter 15   Far Away from the Crowd / 81

Chapter 16   Pastor / 93

Chapter 17   My Biggest Personal Battle / 99

Chapter 18   Nothing to Everything / 106

Foreword

It has been well said that, by and large, 'we are the products of our choices.' And that is a very good reason not only to make wise choices, but to make our first choice in all matters the One who is Wisdom incarnate. It was He who uttered those words of profound wisdom, 'but seek *first* the kingdom of God and his righteousness, and all these things will be added to you.'

It is that choice to seek Him that joins us to His life, to His purpose and to the '*all these things*' of which He spoke—things of material importance as well as the things our deep-heart pines for; things which only He is capable of delivering in their rightful time, place and priority as we go forward, seeking first His kingdom and righteousness.

Whilst our own choices have outcomes that affect our lives for good or ill, what of those things we did not choose, yet which, nevertheless, cause us serious pain and debilitation—choices made by others?

Even then, I believe the above principle still holds true because it is a promise from the only One who never fails or disappoints—and who is a Redeemer. To seek Him first and to get to know Him, brings us into an entirely new strata of existence. A place where He can begin to properly repair damage done to us by others and damage from our own mistakes. It's not a place of total immunity from difficulties but rather one of security—the security of His own presence within us. He walks with us through the tough places of life and in them, delivers to us His peace and wisdom and even great joy. It's the place where He can act in our behalf and for our good.

The curse of Clinical Depression is a malady that can be the result of our own poor choices, or a result of the choices of others during our lives, or even before we were born. Such is the case of my friend Paul Cummings, born 'out of wedlock' as the old and somewhat stigmatizing phrase expressed it. Paul, in this book, has bared his soul about the hidden impacts on his life and takes us with him on his journey from darkness that dogged him and into light that he had not known existed. Patiently and lovingly, the One who he began to seek first, steered Paul's life steps, even when he had no idea how it was happening. Frequently changes and direction came suddenly, yet bore the unmistakable fingerprints of God, to whom Paul had entrusted his life.

Mistakes? Plenty. Frailty? Much…but in what turns out to be an encouragement to seekers and believers alike, Paul's sometimes ordinary and sometimes extraordinary journey shows what God can do, especially in profound healing of deep and even unrecognized pain and damage.

—IAN HEARD

Sydney, Australia

www.until-we-see.com

Preface

A t first, it seemed as if I became a Christian accidently. Time taught
that was not so. God wanted fellowship. I just failed to recognize it.
However, I discovered the God who dwells in heaven is the God who desires to dwell in human hearts. Accepting God's offer of forgiveness has
been the defining moment of my life. I can't take any credit for it. God
pursued me and refused to give up on me. At the right hour, God accepted
me instantly, without reservation.

I became a Christian over forty-five years ago, and this book is testi-
mony to some of what God has done in my life during that time. I've tried
to keep it simple and hope that the reader recognizes, not so much my life,
but God at work.

My walk with God has been like the renovation of a house. Little by
little, year upon year, God would renovate areas of my heart to bring renewal. I call them internal miracles that only God can do.

Much of what God did in my heart was done in a brief moment of
time, hence the title of this book. Though God might, at times, seem far
away, it only takes a moment, a twinkling of an eye, for God to change
people and circumstances. That has been my experience.

I hope you read my little book and see that God met with me through
good times, and bad, success, and failure. In my despair and godless ways,
God remained faithful to me. I can never repay God for such acts of love
and kindness toward me. The least I can offer is praise, worship, and thank-
fulness and the surrendering of my life.

As you read, I pray you may encounter God afresh, to strengthen and
encourage your faith in Jesus.

—PAUL CUMMINGS

Acknowledgments

Chris, for her encouragement to get this book written.

Ian Heard, for his friendship, writing the foreword, and support with my manuscript.

Jinny L Rodman for her editing skills and insights.

Introduction

There is a wonderful scripture in First Corinthians which says: "In a flash, in the twinkling of an eye, at the last trumpet. For the trumpet will sound, the dead will be raised imperishable, and we will be changed." (I Cor. 15:52 NIV)

I know the scripture speaks of a time in the unfolding future of biblical prophecy, but I just love the expression, "in the twinkling of an eye". To me, it conveys a sense of waiting, anticipation, and being still—and then in what seems like all at once, in a single flash, in that 'twinkling' moment—things change. And I don't just mean in my imagination at some distant future in biblical prophecy; my life with God has been marked by many 'twinkling' moments. Moments where God has been changing the old me, renewing my heart, redeeming and directing it in ways that only He could, to become a life transformed by the power of God. It must be said that none of it was against my will, but was often after journeys in wilderness wastelands, and wrestling with God to come to a realization he was serious about my life! Therefore, the best thing I could do was to surrender to him. Sadly, I didn't always distinguish myself with outstanding obedience, humility, and service. There were times of flinging objects around the room, telling God if he wanted them he could have them. There were many times of doing my best to ignore his quiet whispering within. And then there was my favorite avoidance technique, to isolate myself physically and emotionally, so no one could reach out and touch me. Fortunately, I was not out of the reach of God, and in some strange and miraculous way, mercy, grace, and love got through to me. I can't brag about how the Lord touched my life. I can only affirm that he desired to touch it in the first place, and continues to do so.

This book is not written to impress nor to prove to the reader what a great Christian I am; no indeed. It is written to encourage others that God still changes lives today. No matter what point of despair or frustration a person may find themself in, God is truly there with them and available to bring renewal, deliverance, and transformation. These are always available because God is always available, and close by and will arrive at exactly the correct time, 'in the twinkling of an eye'.

Thank you my heavenly father for loving me so much that you sent your only son. Thank you, lord Jesus Christ for dying for me, and restoring me to my heavenly father. Thank you, Holy Spirit for accepting me exactly as I was and for revealing Christ in me.

Chapter 1

Beginnings

I didn't always believe in God. I would often tell people that I was an atheist. It was somewhat strange that I didn't believe in God, really. I know now that God kept reaching out to me to get my attention. I now believe without a shadow of a doubt that God reaches out to people in timely and various ways.

When I was in my late teens, towards turning twenty, I used to walk across some barren land adjacent to an old coal mine to get to work. It was a miserable place to walk and was often made worse with rain, mud, and a freezing crosswind. It could be like that any time of the year, on a bad day. There was an old, broken down moss-covered sandstone wall at the other side and, at times, I used to sit on it on my way back home at the end of my miserable eight hour work day. I would interrupt my journey to just sit there and look at the view tumbling down over the farmer's fields and the countryside. I loved that view, and just looking at it seemed to bring a sense of awe to my miserable life. It really was not much of a view, but compared to the coal mine and barren land, it was beautiful to me. I just used to sit there and think, "there has to be more to all this." The "all this" I referred to, was my general existence, and the life I lived, which was generally spent trudging along my always boring days. I didn't know then what the "more" was, or even what it could be. But, why did I have these thoughts? Where did they come from? Why did I care? Was I looking for meaning and purpose? Could the 'more' be God or a new relationship or just some fun in my life?

Just a few years earlier when I was fifteen, I'd had a strange experience that came totally out of the blue. In our first year at high school, all the students were given a Bible. It was a big thick Bible, which, for some reason, I treasured. I really looked after it and protected it from damage. I never read it, just treasured it. Then all of a sudden, one day I was sitting in the lounge room and had an eerie feeling come over me. For some reason I could not explain, I ran upstairs to my bedroom, grabbed the Bible and tore it into shreds. I totally destroyed it. It was as if I had to destroy it. I felt a strange sort of peace after doing it and was relaxed again. A few days later, I discovered that my Religious Education teacher at high school had been caught in the old local cemetery with her daughters, practicing satanic rituals. Did that have something to do with my tearing up the Bible she had personally put in my hand? I did not know, but it was a distinct possibility. But why did I treasure the Bible when I would tell people I didn't believe in God?

As a child, I had two failed Sunday School experiences. I went to St. Peters Church of England with my best friend, Philip, and that day, the regular attendees, like Philip, got a special book and stickers. I was not allowed to have one because I was new. Because I didn't get one, it was not only the first time I went to that Sunday School, but also the last. Because of a family I knew, I also went to another very small church, the name of which I can't recall. I managed to attend the church for perhaps three times before I stopped going, because all the other kids seemed to get a turn to hold something or read something, and I never did. Following those two experiences, I certainly did not want to go to a church again.

Probably, my strangest childhood experience was, when I was about ten years old. It was the day the Jehovah's Witnesses knocked on our door and announced there was going to be a special meeting down in the village, and we were invited to attend. This had my household buzzing with interest, and questioning if this might be a true religion to follow. Don't ask me why, but I dogmatically told my family I would go to the meeting and check it all out. Strangely enough, when the day came for the meeting, they let me go. The gathering was in the room above the old printer's shop and would hold, I guess, around seventy or eighty people. I found a seat about half way down the center aisle on the right hand side of the room, and about three seats in. I sat there waiting and eventually a man got up and started speaking and describing the religion. I'm not sure how long I listened, but I guess it was somewhere between ten to fifteen minutes. I was not sure about the particular thing the man had said, but somehow I knew immediately that what he was saying was not right. Again, don't ask me how: I just knew.

I stood up and made my way to the aisle with the man's eyes fixed on me as the only person moving around. He had a worried look on his face as I headed for the exit and I sensed he knew I was not impressed. I walked out of the meeting and went straight home. I walked into the house and said to my family, "They are wrong. Don't have anything to do with them." And they never did. How could I do that? A ten-year-old boy, listening to a religious talk for a few minutes and deciding the religion was wrong?

Maybe it had something to do with my "Jesus books" as I called them. They were my only personal retreat and comfort zone. In my bedroom, there was a big box, an old thing with a loose lid because the hinges could no longer hold it, and this was where I kept my Jesus books. There were six or seven books that had been bought for me by a young lady who worked with my mother. Every Christmas, the lady would give me a book that had to do with God and the Bible. I loved those books. If I ever was having a sad day, and that was often for me, I would go and pull out my pile of Jesus books and just sit with them. I was never much of a reader at the best of times, so I would flick through the books and look at the many pictures. Somehow, I would feel comforted. Why would I find comfort in a pile of books about God and Jesus? What drew me to them for comfort?

The only other thing I could remember doing as a child that was anything like religious, was drawing Jesus on the cross. I would spend hours trying to draw the perfect cross and the perfect Jesus. Even Mom would question why I did it so often. I never had a particular reason, other than that I enjoyed doing it.

That's about the sum of my personal religious experiences growing up, other than Religious Education at school, for which I generally received low marks and was perceived on my report as having some interest, but it was not reflected in the standard of my work. Did I learn a lot from those lessons? Was God speaking to me in ways I did not understand?

There was, however, a potentially significant religious moment over my life that my mother told me about. It seems that when I was born, Mom stayed in a halfway house for unmarried mothers and the nurses there used to talk to my mom about Jesus and would even ask Mom to invite Jesus into her life. Apparently, they would also pray for me, that God would protect and guide my life and that one day I would get to know Jesus personally.

How was it I had these moments in my life, even as a baby before I understood anything especially, as I later professed that I did not believe in God? As I honestly reflect on these facts now, I have no answer other than the belief that God reaches out to people and touches lives in ways we may not recognise or understand. But why me? Why did I have these experiences? What did they mean for my life?

To answer all my searching questions, and to find any true meaning in any of them, I have to return to the prayers of the nurses in my first few days and weeks of life; and, to the fact that at age twenty, just a few weeks before my twenty-first birthday, their prayers were about to be answered.

Chapter 2

Poorboy Club

"I will give you a new heart and put a new spirit in you;
I will remove from you your heart of stone and give you a heart of flesh."

(EZEKIEL 36:26 NIV)

I was looking for something in my life, but I had no idea what it was. Well, at the time, to be perfectly honest, I was looking for something and did not even know that I was looking. I now realize that I was looking for meaning and purpose because, in my mind I had no significant reason to exist. Life was just one miserable day after another, with no real purpose other than to try and have enough money in my pocket to buy a drink and play snooker (a game that is similar to billiards). I'd had the thought early in life, that if things ever got too bad, I would just kill myself. In a weird sort of way, I derived a lot of comfort from that thought. The way I saw it, would anyone care at all if I was dead or alive? I'd been that way most of my life, even from childhood, so now, standing on the edge of twenty-one, I saw no encouraging life prospects. Even one of my mates, calling me by my nickname, used to say, "Cumbo, you're not happy unless you're miserable." He hit the nail on the head.

So, here I was, sitting on the train to London, after having had a stroke of genuine good luck. I had walked into my local club just as the barmaid and a friend of mine, Carol, was heading out to play bingo at the local bingo hall. After a quick chat, we decided to go halves. I would pay half the cost of the bingo tickets and any winnings would be shared. This proved to be a good move by me, as Carol won the jackpot, three-hundred-pounds sterling (US$700), cash! My job paid around eighteen pounds per week, so getting my hands on my share of one-hundred-and fifty-pounds (US$350) was quite a windfall for me. My apprenticeship had fallen through after two-and-a-half years, due to the nationwide recession at the time in England. In addition, the steel manufacturing industry in Sheffield, on which a lot of my work relied, collapsed. Decent work was difficult to find, and so, since losing my apprenticeship, I had worked a few mundane and mind-destroying jobs. I was quick to learn that bending steel pipes and digging ditches was not for me. I lasted about six weeks doing those jobs. I had tried being a storeman, receiving and issuing machinery parts for a heavy vehicles workshop with some degree of success, and I was now working in a small engineering manufacturing workshop, as a fitter and turner, mainly on a centre lathe and milling machine making components for industry. It wouldn't be a big decision to leave this job, either. In fact, it was an easy decision now that I had one-hundred-and-fifty-pounds in my pocket to do with as I wished.

It was an easy choice for me to make. I decided to take some time out in London to ease the pain of facing normal, everyday life. My friends were not sure if I was brave or just plain crazy to take the 200 mile trip to London by myself. I figured it was no big deal. I had done this before. I liked London. It was not hard, given I absolutely hated any job I found myself in and was always looking to leave and have a good time elsewhere. One-hundred and fifty pounds was not a lot of money, but I figured I could survive a few days in relatively good accommodation and have a few nights on the town as well. A bit corny, I know but to me, one-hundred-and-fifty-pounds spelt, sex, drugs, and rock-and-roll.

I didn't do it very often, but I did always enjoy the train ride from Sheffield to Kings Cross St. Pancras Railway Station in London. Sitting, watching the world go by, I could just look out at the scenery and allow my thoughts to wander wherever I wanted them to. For some reason, I have always liked to sit and think. We were, however, living in troubled times in England. I frequently looked at the luggage racks for security reasons. If a bag was left on the luggage rack without good reason, the train guard had to be notified because of the danger of a possible Irish Republican Army (IRA) bomb attack. It always paid to check the luggage racks every time the train stopped at a station and then restarted its journey. I once made the mistake of going to the Restaurant Car at the wrong time, only to return to my seat to find guards anxiously discussing what to do with my luggage. It was all dealt with amicably, but people in the train car had been worried.

Turning my gaze from the window, my eyes made one of their customary trips to the luggage racks above my head in front of me. I had done this many times, but this time I exposed myself to an unusual experience. As I glanced up at the luggage rack, it was as if there was a hole straight through it, and much more than that. It looked as though the luggage rack, together with the roof of the train, had been torn open. There was, what appeared to be, a hole with torn and bent mental around the edge, similar to what you see in a Superhero comic when they'd punched a car or water tank. Through the hole, I could see what appeared to be the normal blue sky with white clouds. From either side of this image entered two characters, one coming from the right and one from the left, as if entering a stage show. I guessed they were two men, but they seemed to be wearing long robes, so it was hard to tell. Within a second, they began to wrestle with each other. I had the distinct impression they were wrestling over the control of something or someone. After gazing at this scene for a while, I had the overwhelming feeling it was me they were fighting over. Strangely enough, I was not particularly concerned or perturbed by it at all. Although I'd never experienced anything like this, rather than being fearful or disturbed by it, I just looked away and out of the window and carried on with my journey, almost as if nothing had happened. At the time, I think the reality of what I had experienced had not really hit me. In fact, it was going to be a week or so before I would get an understanding of what it all meant. In that brief moment, I dismissed it as soon as I looked away.

As the train passed the Watford Football Ground, I knew it was nearly time to disembark, so I made myself ready. In London, I always felt a sense of freedom and adventure. It was good to be back.

I found a place to stay in a boarding house where I could pay one day at a time. That suited me, as I did not know from one day to the next what I would be doing. I had a nice room with a single bed, wardrobe (I'd never had a wardrobe) and a small dresser. It was pretty drab, but it looked good to me. My first day in London was spent seeing a few of the tourist sites and enjoying some pubs. My second day was pretty much the same until the evening came. I decided, as I saw it, to begin to enjoy myself on a different level. I set out from my digs to find a suitable pornographic movie theater. The truth was, any would be suitable. I found a place promising the fulfilment for all my desires, paid my fee and took a seat. The place was packed.

There were a couple of movies to be seen and I watched the first eagerly and happily, but my eagerness and happiness took a sudden downward turn during the second movie. I began to feel decidedly uncomfortable, and I started looking around at all the others gathered there. It seemed really strange. Just about everyone was leaning forward in their seat with their eyes and tongue hanging out, yet I felt increasingly uneasy. I began to feel "dirty" on the inside. I'd never felt like this before. It was as if I suddenly had the internal knowledge that I was doing wrong by being in this theater. My feelings of doing wrong and guilt only increased during the next movie. As the second movie finished, I made my way to the exit. As I pushed my way through the swinging exit doors, the blinding light hit me right in the eyes and the heart. The foyer of the theater had bright lights all around the edge of the ceiling and, as I walked from the dark theater into the bright lights, it was as if those lights were shining through to the inside of me and casting light on the darkness within. I didn't really know what was happening, but I sure felt dirty on the inside. My conscience began to bother me and I felt unclean and alone. Later, I learnt I was experiencing a conviction of my sin. Keeping my head down, I made my way through the foyer and down the front steps and onto the main street.

Still feeling perturbed, I was distracted from my thoughts by a young woman suddenly appearing on the pavement in front of me, slapping a piece of paper in my hand and saying,

"Jesus loves you, and I love you too!"

My feelings of uncleanness were quickly cast aside as I considered this was an opportunity too good to miss. Love was what I wanted, and for me, it was better spelled as *sex*. I figured I was onto a good thing and did not want to let the chance slip by. I began to try to "chat up" the girl and tried to get her to have a drink with me, but this was to no avail as she had to catch the tube train home. However there was hope for me and the chance of success on another day. This came in the shape of the Poorboy Club coffee shop. Her name was Miriam and once she told me about the coffee shop, I arranged to meet her there on the next Friday evening. We said our goodbyes and went our separate ways and I could not believe my good luck as I clung on to the Poorboy Club's address. Journeying home, I could only think about seeing Miriam again in the very near future.

The next morning, I awoke with Miriam on my mind. It was Wednesday, and I figured there just might be the possibility that the Poorboy Club could be open that night, so I decided to use my time that day to find my way there. The address was Finchley Road, and it would be easy to find by tube train and bus. Eventually, boarding a Finchley Road bus, I asked the conductor to let me know when I was near the number I wanted. Finchley Road seemed to go on forever, the longest road I think I had ever encountered. After what seemed like an age, I reckoned the conductor must have forgotten about my request, so I exited at the next bus stop. It turned out to be not so clever a move, as it ended up taking me about another three quarters of an hour of walking before I reached my destination. The club was closed when I arrived, but a sign on the door showed that it would be open later at 7:00 pm. It was now 5:30 pm, so I decided to find a place to eat. I found a cafe just up the road from the club where I could see the club's front door from my window seat. While I was still eating and sipping my cup of tea, someone arrived early to open up the club, which meant once I'd finished my meal, I wouldn't have to hang around on the street waiting for the place to open.

As I walked in the front doorway of the club, I was confronted with a flight of narrow stairs and the sound of laughter coming from somewhere unseen, upstairs. As I reached the top of the stairs, they took a sharp turn left and led me onto a narrow hallway about 5 meters, or approximately 15 feet long. In the hallway, were two guys talking and laughing with each other. "We're not open yet," said the taller of the two guys as he headed for the room at the other end of the hallway. I think my arrival had reminded them that they should be setting up the place and not standing around talking and laughing.

"Hi," said the other guy left standing there, "I'm Sammy," he continued, as he reached out to shake my hand. He was about the same height as me with a shock of fair hair and a short but bushy reddish-colored beard. His smile was the broadest I had ever seen, and his eyes had a real sparkle to them. His eyes met mine as he reached out his hand, which was all very confronting to me. I took his hand and introduced myself but allowed my eyes to wander anywhere rather than look into his. I was quite taken aback by his apparent willingness to talk to me. He came across as sincere and genuinely interested in me. While we spoke, he stepped into a small booth built into the wall of the hallway, which happened to be the ticket office. As we continued talking, people were entering the coffee shop and Sammy was taking a fifty-pence entry fee from each of them. I told him about my encounter with Miriam the night before and that I was hoping to see her that evening. He told me that he did not think Miriam would be there until

Friday, but that there was another girl I could talk to if I wanted. I thought that sounded really good and I remember thinking, this was my sort of place because if one girl is not available, they provide another one! I'd not laid eyes on the girl but I figured what the heck, any port in a storm, right? Sammy said he would let me in without paying the fifty-pence (US$1.20¢) entry fee if I could not afford it. Even though I would have preferred not to pay, I paid it anyway, in fairness to how kind Sammy had been to me.

As no one else was waiting to pay, Sammy took me into the room at the end of the hallway, which happened to be a dingy coffee shop with some background music playing. Just inside the room, a guy and a girl were standing and chatting, so Sammy introduced me to them. They both seemed friendly and genuinely happy to meet me. The girl's name was Rachel, and she suggested that the two of us sit at a table and have a coffee. I readily agreed with this suggestion, thinking to myself that this was all just too good to be true. We moved to the far end of the coffee shop, into a small alcove sort of room, away from the music speakers and sat together on a bench seat. Instead of coffee, we ended up having a couple of cans of soft drink.

Rachel took a chain from around her neck with a pendant on it and asked me, "Do you know what this pendant is?" I held it in my hand, and to me, it looked like a key ring. I figured that would be the wrong answer so rather than make myself sound dumb, I just said, "No."

"It's a Yoke of Love," she replied. "We sell them", she said as she pointed in the direction where others were placed ready to be purchased. She raved on about how people could be yoked together through love. It all seemed a pretty dumb idea to me, but I kept listening in a polite sort of way. "Do you read the Bible?" enquired Rachel. Now this was where I figured I would really impress her. I reached into my jacket pocket and pulled out a small Bible, about 2.5 centimetres, or just about an inch, square, as I said, "This is the smallest New Testament in the world and I use it as a good luck charm"—which, strangely enough, was absolutely true.

At this stage in my life, I had made the decision to call myself an atheist. The fact that I had this Bible in my pocket, was due to a girl at school giving it to me in a swap deal; it had nothing to do with any religious inclination on my behalf. After all, how many people could boast of carrying the smallest Bible in the world around with them? I just kept it in my pocket, and whenever I was in any sort of need, I would grab hold of it and make a wish that things would work out for me. Strangely enough, that seemed to work for me. In hindsight, I believe it was more than just plain good luck. I think God was looking after me even then.

Much to my chagrin, my Bible didn't seem to cause her to bat an eyelid, let alone impress her. She made a little comment about the Bible, but asked, "Do you believe in God?"

My response surprised me. "Yes", I said. I wasn't sure why I said "Yes." I had publicly declared my atheism a number of times so now why was I saying, "Yes"?

As the thoughts went through my mind, I remember saying to myself, "God, if you are listening, I don't really believe in you, I'm only saying this to get somewhere with this girl." (I was unsure how I could talk to a God I said did not exist).

"Do you know that God loves you?," asked Rachel, as she looked for the answer in my eyes. I remained silent.

My silence did not deter her, as the story unfolded from her lips of a God who had given his life for all the wrong things I had done, and that he had done so because he loves me.

I must say, I didn't understand much of what Rachel was saying, but she had gained my full attention. Continuing, she spoke of Jesus and His love for me, even though I had done bad things.

"Do you believe you have done wrong things in your life, Paul"? Now, this really did begin to ring bells on the inside of me. Mainly, because my experience at the movie theater had made me realize that I was dirty on the inside—not that I understood what a feeling like that really meant for me. Rachel explained to me that the wrong things that I'd done were what the Bible called "sin" and that these were the very things that separated me from God, and was the reason Jesus had died. Then Rachel spoke of something that caused me to have a sense of hope within me; God's forgiveness.

She explained how God wanted to forgive me and have a relationship with me, but it was up to me to ask him, God would not force himself upon me. "Do you ever pray?" she asked. Again, I was put on the spot with a question to which I wanted to answer "No", but I knew deep inside that if I was honest, it demanded a "yes" answer. I begrudgingly squeezed out a "Yes." It was hard for me, as it was a sort of confession and a very personal thing to share with a stranger. Not to mention, my personal confusion at realizing that I did pray, or at least talked to someone or something I reckoned didn't exist! Rachel seemed to be getting excited as the next question flowed from her lips. In my entire life, I don't think anyone had ever asked me so many personal questions like the ones Rachel asked.

"Would you like to pray to God now and ask Him to forgive you for all the things you have done wrong,"? I opened my mouth to answer, but before I could say anything, her next question emerged.

"Then you could ask Jesus to come and live in your heart, to be your personal lord and savior. Would you like to do that?" Rachel's face was beaming as she asked, as if she knew something I didn't. And she did.

I did not understand all that Rachel was saying, but for some strange reason, I said I was willing to pray, but that I had no idea what to say. I figured this gave me a way out. I figured wrong. At the very least this girl was persistent!

"I'll pray, and you use the words I use but say them from your heart to God." I was cornered with no way out, so I just said, "Yes."

Rachel took the lead.

"Let's just bow our heads and close our eyes," she said. "Just repeat this prayer after me, a little at a time."

As I bowed my head and closed my eyes, I said a sort of silent prayer before Rachel even started to pray. I didn't think it was a real prayer at the time, it was more of a quick chat to God. In the silence of my heart, I said, "God I'm going to pray to you now, but I have to be honest and tell you that I'm not sure you are really there."

Rachel began to pray with me repeating her words.

"Dear Living God."

"Dear Living God."

"I admit I have done wrong things."

"I admit I have done wrong things."

"I know you call these wrong things, sin."

"I know you call these wrong things, sin."

"I accept that Jesus died for all my sins."

"I accept that Jesus died for all my sins."

"I now ask you to forgive me for all that I have done wrong."

"I now ask you to forgive me for all that I have done wrong."

"And for all the sins I have committed."

"And for all the sins I have committed."

"I believe that Jesus rose from the dead."

"I believe that Jesus rose from the dead."

"And is alive today."

"And is alive today."

"And I ask you now Lord Jesus."

"And I ask you now Lord Jesus."

"To come into my heart."

"To come into my heart."

"And be my personal lord and savior."

"And be my personal lord and savior."

"Amen."

"Amen."

As I opened my eyes, I saw Rachel with a big smile on her face, looking eagerly at me as if she was expecting something to happen to me. And happen, it did! I could not believe it, but I had to, because it was really happening. It began to happen as soon as I said "Amen." As the word left my lips, I immediately began to feel different on the inside. My heart felt touched, and seemed like it was going to burst. It was as if my heart was growing and my chest was expanding. I felt a change in my head too, as my mind felt clear and at peace. A welling up seemed to rise from my heart, up to my head and a smile came upon my face which I could not seem to control. I had an incredible sense of joy exploding in my heart! I was changed, and I felt love inside me and it all happened in such an instant. It was only days later that I began to realize and understand something of what I was experiencing. Needless to say, this was new to me and way beyond any experience I had ever had. Before this moment, I honestly don't think I had ever felt peace, joy, and love before. Maybe I knew about them in my head, but this was all coming from my heart! "How was that?" asked Rachel, with a look of anticipation on her face. I opened my mouth to answer her, but no words would come out. I just had a beaming smile and an incredible sense of joy. My speech was gone, and replaced by joy unbridled. I literally could not speak. I tried really hard to, but all I could do was laugh and offer gestures signifying that my heart was full. I motioned with my hands on my chest, something had changed on the inside but I was not able to communicate it with words.

For the first time in my life, I was experiencing love unbounded. I had an incredible awareness that Jesus was in my heart and that God was indeed alive! I discovered later that I was experiencing what is called being "born again." This is when we give our life to God, and then his Holy Spirit comes to dwell within us. When God enters our life, our lost relationship with him is restored.

Rachel took me over to Sammy and another guy who had turned up, and whom I later found out was their leader. "Tell them what has just happened to you, Paul." Again, I opened my mouth to speak, but no words came out, just more speechless joy expressed in laughter and heavy sighs which sounded like I was having breathing problems, more than anything else. The three of them just laughed with me and seemed overjoyed at my newfound experience. I lost all sense of time during the rest of the evening and just immersed in my newfound joy. I remember we locked up the coffee shop and were walking to a car to take me to the tube station, when a lady appeared out of nowhere selling small bunches of flowers. I had no money for flowers, but I took her by the hand and started to dance with her in the street while telling her how much God loved her! She just laughed at what I had to say.

On arrival at the tube station, I arranged with Sammy and Rachel to meet them at the Poorboy Club on Friday night. We then hugged, which was new to me, and I disappeared into the tube station. Standing alone on the platform, I was still overcome with joy and smiling to myself. Trains came and went, and it suddenly dawned on me that I must be sticking out like a sore thumb.

I prayed, "Lord, I must look a proper idiot standing here smiling at nothing. You better take it away or people will think I am a nut case." But it did not go away. I arrived at the boarding house quite late and quietly made my way to my room. I was very tired, so I quickly got ready for bed, turned off the light and jumped between the sheets. I had discovered what I was looking for in life. It was God all along. I was now a born again believer with a heart of flesh, rather than one of stone. This is what God had promised hundreds of years before in the book of Ezekiel, "I will give you a new heart and put a new spirit within in you; I will remove from you your heart of stone and give you a heart of flesh." (Ezekiel 36:26 NIV)

It was the most amazing feeling and experience I ever had. It still is. God stepped into my life, in the twinkling of an eye. "Jesus replied, "Very truly, I tell you, no one can see the kingdom of God unless they are born again." (John 3:3 NIV)

Chapter 3

Jesus Lovers or Jesus Cult?

Friday came around quickly, and I again found myself in the Poorboy Club talking to Sammy. We had something in common now; we both knew Jesus. Miriam, the girl I had met outside the movies earlier that week, arrived and seemed interested in me, and I shared my news with her. She was over the moon with excitement for me, and listened with keenness to my story of meeting Jesus. After she had heard my story, Miriam moved on to talk with others. She didn't seem that interested in me for the remainder of the evening.

My life had changed drastically because of these people whose company I was now enjoying, but I had no idea who they were or where they came from. That was about to change. The leader, who was there the night I was born again, came up to me and asked me when my birthday was. For some reason, I felt uneasy and vulnerable in his presence. He was tall and slim, with dark features and a constant thoughtful look on his face, as if he was always thinking about what he would say or do next. His name was Peter. "Second of February," I answered. This seemed to excite Peter and caused something of a stir among the group. It turned out that my birthday fell on the same day as that of the International Leader of their religious group, a guy who called himself Moses David. It was at this point that I discovered that this band of people were all members of what was called the Children of God. I discovered later, that they were classed as a sect. This did not freak me out too much at the time, as they had led me to Jesus and I was feeling the happiest I had ever been in my life. Even though I had no idea who the Children of God really were, for some reason I was a bit perturbed and suspicious regarding all the fuss about my birthday. I just reckoned that a person's birthday should be no big deal to God. I did not share my thoughts with anyone at the time though, and just hid them in my heart.

Surprisingly, Peter invited me to live with the group at a house they were squatting in at Hampstead Heath. As I was quickly running out of money, and was due to leave the boarding house the next morning, I considered his offer too good to refuse.

The next morning, I found myself knocking on the door of the biggest house I had ever seen normal people live in. It was amazing to my eyes. I had been brought up in a small, semi-detached council house in South Yorkshire, and this was light years away from there. I could not believe it, as Sammy opened the door. I was genuinely happy to see him, and in the short time I had known him, it seemed like he was becoming a dear friend. As I stepped inside, I was taken aback by the size and timbered decor of the entrance area. I'd never seen anything like it. This led into a large hall with an imposing dark, wooden staircase on the left-hand side. I had never seen so much elegant woodwork in a house. There were people milling around everywhere and it all seemed very busy. Sammy introduced me to people as they passed by us. There were far too many names for me to remember. "We all have been given a name from the Bible," said Sammy. "I'm Sammy from the word, Samaritan." I thought that sounded a bit silly, but I didn't say anything. "If you stay with us, you will receive one too." I made no comment, but I thought my name was fine just as it was. Peter appeared at the top of the stairs on the landing. It seemed obvious now that he was the leader as he was like a general marshalling his troops. All seemed to be looking to him for direction.

I had arrived at a time when the whole household was preparing to hit the streets for evangelism. I did not understand what this meant, but Peter invited me to be involved and explained his expectations to me. Apparently, each person received what they called Mo Letters. These were small booklets that had been written by Moses David and were seen as important messages for the group to learn from. Evangelism meant to take the Mo Letters to the streets and generally give them away while telling people about God. If at all possible, money should be gained in exchange. This would provide funds on which the group would survive.

I was given about 50 booklets, but I was so keen I insisted on taking more, so I ended up with about 100 of them and a sincere belief that I might still not have enough. We were split up into teams and I was with Rachel and a guy I had just met, called Thomas. All the teams left the house and made their way to their designated destinations.

We had to catch a bus and once we were at our destination, I was left with no doubt as to what I had to do. Rachel and Thomas would thrust their hand, complete with a Mo Letter in front of people walking down the street. If a person tried to take one, they were engaged in conversation and encouraged to offer a donation. If the conversation could lead to talking about God, then all the better. I saw many responses from people throughout the day. Most people just kept walking as if nothing was offered to them. A few were eager to get hold of a Mo Letter and make a suitable donation. Still others, especially youth, were open to chatting, mainly about God with questions about life and death. Few seemed to ask who The Children of God were. Thomas was a tall, attractive guy in his early twenties and seemed to target talking to girls. At one point, he was surrounded by four teenage girls and was merrily chatting away with them. In contrast, Rachel seemed to target young men.

I did not do a lot that day. I mainly just tagged along and observed. When I did manage to engage someone in conversation, Rachel and Thomas were usually on hand to take control of the situation.

We arrived home four hours later and, as I walked in the door, Peter greeted me with a broad smile and a question. "So Paul, how many Mo Letters did you manage to distribute today?" This was embarrassing for me, as there were quite a few people standing around waiting for my answer. "Two", I said, lowering my eyes to the ground. "Well done", said Peter as he put his arm enthusiastically around my shoulder. "That's two more than the church," he quipped to the delight of his audience. "And how much money did you raise?"

"Three shillings," (US .80¢) I said excitedly. I knew it wasn't much but from just two people I thought it was great! Peter and the crowd gave a cheer and laughed as if I had won a victory of some sort. Others began to share what they had done until we were interrupted with the announcement that dinner was being served in the dining room. After dinner, I was shown to the bedroom, which was more like an army barracks, with about 15 single beds in the one room. I was given the bed of a guy who was away at the time, and was once the lead guitarist for a band which had a number-one hit in the U.K. charts. From what I could work out, he was not part of The Children of God group but stayed with them often.

The next morning, I arose to the arrival of the lead guitarist, who was pretty annoyed that I had slept in his bed, given that I had left it in a mess. He confronted me angrily face to face. I was embarrassed enough that this had happened, let alone the whole household hearing him shouting at me. He was angry with me for a while because of it, but we parted amicably, eventually.

After breakfast, I was handed over to a young man, called Michael, who took me away into a room together with a Bible. We sat down in a massive room, and he began to read and explain the Bible to me. To be honest, none of what he was saying to me seemed to be making sense. I wasn't sure if it was him, me, or the Bible's fault. Every so often, Peter would pop his head around the door and ask Michael how things were going. I felt like I was being tested.

At the end of my Bible study, I was handed over to another guy, called Paul, who took me for a walk on Hampstead Heath, which was close to where we were staying. It was just a large parkland area, and we walked and chatted for an hour or so. I was not sure if it was my imagination or not, but I had the distinct feeling I was not being allowed to be by myself. It also seemed to me that whoever I spent time with wanted to know about my personal financial position and my family life. Neither of these subjects rose to any great heights at that time in my life. I had five pounds and a return train ticket to Sheffield left in all the world and my mother had written to me saying she could not manage with my unstable lifestyle, and that it might be best if I left home permanently. These things did not worry me too much as I could always go on unemployment if I needed money, and I never did what my mother wanted.

Paul and I returned to the house where on arrival, Peter took me to one side for a chat together with Sammy. Peter told me I would not be able to remain with the group. I was not surprised to hear this. Somehow, I felt that I had failed the test of the group. I was not the sort of person to just accept the things people told me on face value without checking things out further. I think my wanting more detailed answers did not impress them. Sammy was disappointed with the news, and looked disbelievingly at Peter. He received a stern look in return and that was enough to prevent Sammy taking it any further. I didn't hang around after that. I was encouraged by Peter to contact a Children of God group in Manchester when I returned home, and Sammy was asked to show me to the door. I felt fine about it all, but I could tell Sammy was upset.

As we said farewell to each other on the doorstep, another new experience for me, as we had a brotherly hug and kissed each other in the neck. As we parted, we both had tears in our eyes. In the short time we had known each other, our relationship was bound with a bond of love in Jesus. God had put something new in my heart and I was acting like a different person with a new life in me. I was never to see Sammy again, but I still think of him and pray for him from time to time, as I do for the others I met there.

It had been the most amazing week of my life and now I was on the train heading back home to Hoyland, the small village I lived in, about thirty minutes drive from Sheffield, in South Yorkshire. As I thought of all that had happened to me, I wondered how friends and family would respond when I told them. Apart from my day work, I also had a part-time job in the evenings as a barman in a Catholic Social Club, and, as I was generally in there nearly every day of my life, I thought I would go there before I went home. I arrived at the club about an hour before closing time on a Sunday evening. As I walked in, a drink was automatically poured for me with my friends eager to know the news from my trip. There was a look of disbelief on their face as I told them. I didn't say too much just that I had found Jesus and that he was God and a real person and that they could get to know Him as well if they wanted to.

I didn't realize it at the time, but I was witnessing to others. One friend reminded me that I had said in the past that the singer David Bowie was God. I said I had been wrong and now I knew that Jesus was God. He said he would remind me one day when the novelty of my new beliefs wore off. He has never had the chance to. As the news went around the club, others invited me to chat with them about my experience. This was really great for me, as although I did not know all the right things to say, I knew Jesus and my excitement about that alone really seemed to challenge people and make them want to listen. I walked home from the club having shared about Jesus with many people and feeling really great about it all. As I reached home, I walked through the side door and into the kitchen to find my mom and my great aunt sitting on the sofa. I could not contain myself, so I blurted out, "I've found Jesus, and He's real." Mom looked at me in a somewhat thoughtful and troubled manner as she replied, "That's good, dear."

We chatted about Jesus for a while and all that had happened to me. Mom was suitably impressed, but concerned about The Children of God, as she had seen something on the television about how they supposedly cheated people out of their money and split families up. She said they were a cult and were dangerous. As I went to bed, I appreciated what Mom had said, but I was still determined to visit the group in Manchester. The next morning I woke up ready to read my 'Mo Letters'. I had quite a few with me and had decided to learn all I could from them. However, I was not impressed with what I read. Even though I did not know much about the Bible, the things I was reading in the letters seemed suspicious to me. There was the booklet, *Flirty Fishing*, which openly encouraged flirting with members of the opposite sex in order to win them to Jesus. As far as I could tell, there was no restriction on how far you could go. Then there was the Mo Letter called, *Holy Holes*, which discussed all the holes in a person's body and why they were there. To me, there seemed to be unhealthy connotations in the letter. I began considering all the comments from the group in the past week and the things which had seemed suspicious to me. It took me a while, but I finally came to a decision not to pursue my involvement with The Children of God. By seeking to discern all that had happened, I believe that God was showing me that this was the right decision to make. But I must sincerely say, I will be eternally grateful that they introduced me to Jesus.

But, I was now confused about what to do as a Christian. In my brief time with The Children of God, they had taught me that the mainline churches were apostate and not living as God wanted them to. I really did not know if I should go to church or not. I knew very little at the time, but it would be five years and only after some life-changing personal encounters with God, before I would ever join a church. But one thing I did know was that Jesus was in my heart and that Jesus Christ was lord.

It was at this point that I remembered, or was reminded by God, of what I had seen when on the train to London; the hole in the roof and the beings wrestling with each other. This was now answered for me. It was two angels fighting over me. They were wrestling over my soul. God wanted me and the Devil didn't want God to get me. The Devil did not want me to hear the gospel of Jesus Christ and God's gift of Salvation. God wanted me to have the chance to hear that message and make my choice. I'm so glad to be able to say, God won!

Chapter 4

Australian Pain and God's Hope

L ife went on much the same for me. I still didn't know a lot about Christianity and what it was really all about. All I knew was that Jesus was in my heart and that when I died I would go to be with Him. That was about the extent of my knowledge. Looking back, I don't fully know how I believed that so strongly, except on the strength of my conversion experience. Apart from believing that, I thought I could do whatever I wanted with the rest of my life. But no, that wasn't the case.

On returning from London, I had managed to get my old job back at the engineering manufacturing workshop. But, when I got too bored, I walked out of that job again. I also quit my job in the bar, as I considered it was ruining my social life. Too often, it seemed all my mates were going out to nightclubs and I would be working behind the bar, watching them walk out of the door, wishing I was with them. As was my usual style, I dropped both jobs without any warning. The week I dropped both jobs, I landed a new girlfriend. Great timing, now I had no money to take her out. Her name was Melanie, and she was on a working holiday for twelve months from Australia. Within the twelve months, we decided that we would one day get married, and we made an application for a visa for me to enter Australia. We had to go to Leeds for an interview and to state our case. It was while in Leeds that the Lord spoke to me clearly in a way I have never forgotten. The interview went well, and we were told I would be granted a visa for entry into Australia, on the provision that we marry within six months from my entry date. That was fine by us, and we left the interview room really excited. We decided to go and find something to eat and do a bit of shopping. However, for some reason, all was not well in my thinking, and I had negative thoughts running around in my head. All at once, I was beginning to question what was happening in my life, searching within myself for answers. I suppose it was because we had just been into a meeting that gave us an answer for a specific direction in our life together, and for me, it immediately kicked off doubts in my head. I said nothing to Melanie, but I was beginning to wonder what God thought about my life, and especially in relation to Melanie.

I had spoken to Melanie about God and, as she was a Catholic, she believed in God and it seemed important to her that I did, too, so much so that, upon marriage, I would be expected to convert to Catholicism. I remember I said I was open to converting, but that was about as far as we ever went with that conversation.

All at once, now in my heart, I was beginning to wonder if Melanie was to be a real part of my life, and eventually become my wife. Going to Australia was a big issue for me too. Did God really want me there? It seemed to me that I had always wanted to live in Australia, even from a young child. I'd always been fascinated with the outlaw, Ned Kelly, who wore the armor to stop bullets, and I loved anything on television that had to do with Australia. But was this how it was supposed to work out? I had no doubt I loved Melanie very much; it was just the enormity of the decision that made me feel somewhat overwhelmed.

Somehow, we found ourselves in an outdoor shopping mall and I bought a magazine and sat on a bench while Melanie went off to find a ladies room. There were not many people around, probably because it was a cold day. I sat with my open magazine and it would have looked to a passerby as if I was reading it. I wasn't, as the thoughts in my head were elsewhere. Was I really doing the right thing? The question would not leave me. While I sat there, miles away in my thoughts, a man suddenly seemed to appear from nowhere and stood in front of me. He stooped down so that his eyes were level with mine and spoke very clearly and succinctly the following words, "The lord says everything will be all right." He kept looking directly into my eyes and continued. "Do you hear what I am saying? The lord says everything will be all right!" "Do you hear me? Everything will be all right. The lord says so." I was away in my thoughts and I was in a bit of a daze, but his eyes remained on mine until I gave him an indication that I had understood what he had said, which I eventually did with a slight nod. He then stood up and walked away. It was as if I came to my senses and in a split second, I turned around to ask him a question. I could not believe it; he was not there. There was no crowd, nowhere for him to hide, he just was not there! As quickly as he had arrived, he vanished. Though I did not fully understand the implications of his words, I had a real sense that the lord had answered the pondering of my heart, 'in the twinkling of an eye'. I took hold of those words as coming from God himself. I had a peace that God was still watching over my life and that he knew what was happening to me. Even more, I felt God had a future for me in Australia. Just then, Melanie returned with a half-smile and a questioning look on her face, asking, "Are you all right?" She must have recognized that I was looking around strangely for some reason. I just mumbled, "Fine," and we carried on with our day.

Though I did not understand any of this at the time, I did later have a distinct sense that I had been visited by an angel from God. Returning to Hoyland, Melanie and I told no one of our intentions to marry, as neither of us liked to have people knowing our business. Whenever I had doubts about moving to Australia, it seemed I was always reminded of the words of the angel, "the lord says everything will be all right." Melanie returned to Australia by herself in early 1976.

I had now gone back to work for my first employer, and though the pay was not great, he did loan me the money for my one-way ticket to Australia. I followed Melanie about six months later. My first night in Australia set the tone for the future of our relationship.

I arrived in Brisbane at around 4:00 pm on a Friday afternoon. It was something of a shock to say the least. When I had arrived at Heathrow Airport in London, I had been confronted with the three biggest buildings I had ever seen in my life. They were massive and the whole airport was beyond my imagination. The jumbo jet was obviously big, and I even got to be the pilot for a few moments as the captain let me have a go on the controls on the way over. But, a huge contrast followed upon landing in Brisbane, where I was greeted by aircraft steps onto the tarmac and had to walk about the length of two football fields to what seemed nothing more than a very large tin shed. The "tin shed" was the Brisbane Airport terminal! It seemed like I'd arrived in some nation truly left behind in the past. Once inside the terminal, I realized it was a bit larger than I first imagined, but it still did not endear me to discovering Brisbane.

I had not told Melanie about my imminent departure from England and my planned arrival time in Brisbane. I went to the bar in the lounge area and started talking with two local guys, one of whom had just put his family on a flight and was already chatting up the barmaid. They were originally from England and we talked football until one of them asked where I was headed to. Somehow in the conversation, one of them did me the service of finding the telephone number for Melanie's workplace. I telephoned Melanie at work. The phone seemed to ring for ages before she answered it, and apparently, I had just caught her on her way out of work; she had to come back to answer the telephone. She couldn't believe I was in Australia. It seemed to put her into a panic, as she was on her way to a twenty-first birthday party. We arranged for her to pick me up at the airport as soon as she could get there. First, she would have to go home and explain the situation to her mother and stepfather and ask if I could stay with them for a few days. The plan went radically wrong when her stepfather, Archie, who was the worse for wear with alcohol, met me in the airport lounge and took me to their home in his sporty Triumph car. It was the most fearful car drive I had ever taken. He was half drunk, speeding, describing everything we sped past, and intent on asking me every question he could about my relationship with Melanie. With every question I answered, he seemed to get angrier at me. I thought he was going to crash the car when I told him Melanie and I were planning on getting married; that was totally unexpected news for his ears. Somehow, we made it home safely. Well, not yet. What I thought was "home" was the Inala Hotel, where he took me for a drink and a chat with one of his mates. He was blatantly talking negatively about me to his friend, and putting me down at every opportunity. He was really shaking his head telling his mate the news of the potential wedding, as if needing some solace to make sense of it all. I won't repeat what his mate said to him, but he certainly got no supportive words.

Due to having never had a father in my own life, and having experienced extensive emotional abuse from a male growing up, I was starting to feel very emotionally fragile and vulnerable. I did not relate to men very well in the best of circumstances, and this was far from pleasant. I was close to tears, but trying to hold it together. I think his mate could see this, and I think it was he who suggested that Archie take me home to Melanie. It only took another two or three minutes of inebriated abuse to get there.

When we got home, Melanie's mom was warm and welcoming but Melanie was not there. Archie had not told anyone he was going to pick me up, so poor Melanie had gone out to the airport only to find I was not there. Melanie turned up about an hour later wondering what had happened to me. Fortunately, I could not be blamed for that one! Well, not fully anyway.

The mood of the house was a little strained, to say the least. Melanie's mom gave Archie a hard time for the rest of the night, and I could not have asked for more. After all, he had not endeared himself to me. To be honest, I was not really bothered about what was happening to Archie, given that Melanie seemed friendly, but somewhat distant with me. I suppose her shell of privacy had been shattered. Melanie and I just talked politely to each other, a sort of diplomatic conversation. Not much was said of my sudden arrival and my overall intentions.

Melanie's view of the night was that a lot had happened, and as it was getting late, maybe we should all sleep on it. Tomorrow would be a new day. They made a bed up on the lounge room floor which was fine by me but I felt they were embarrassed by their lack of proper accommodation.

I felt very confused on the inside. As I lay my head on the pillow, I began to cry. It seemed obvious to me that Melanie was no longer interested in our relationship, and I was really hurt from the way her stepfather treated me. I was thirteen-thousand-miles from home, and no longer had my mom and the home I had always known, to fall back on. I felt incredibly alone and vulnerable. And yet at this point in time as I lay there, I had this incredible sense that I was where God wanted me to be. It was as if God was providing me with an inner spiritual peace, even though otherwise, I felt I was struggling. I prayed through my tears,

"Jesus, I don't understand why I am here, but I know you want me here. I just ask that you help me sort all this out, amen." Still sobbing, I fell asleep.

Within my first week, I found a job as a fitter and turner at a small workshop called Zenith Engineering in Milton, an inner suburb of Brisbane. I was due to start work on just my second Monday in Australia. I stayed with Melanie's family until the Saturday before I started work. I moved into the Kingsley Private Hotel on George Street in Brisbane City, at a cost of twenty-five dollars per week for a single room and shared kitchen, laundry, television room, etc.

Melanie had made it very clear in that first week that there was no way we were going to be married, ever! I was very upset to say the least. It wasn't so much that we would not be together, but more the sense of rejection that grieved me. Somehow, on the inside I knew we should not be together. I still had a sense that everything would be fine as told me by the angel, and a sense within, that God wanted me in Australia. I was hurting deeply though.

The sense of rejection was overwhelming. I had no friends, and the few acquaintances I had only laughed at me as they reckoned I talked funny with my Yorkshire accent. I dealt with things the only way I knew how, through alcohol and women. I drank at every opportunity and I soon had a reputation for being found on the floor of the shared kitchen at the hotel. I would sleep with any woman I could find, without looking for any sort of ongoing relationship. I just wanted to feel wanted. Drugs also became a problem in my life in the form of marijuana. I had always said I would never take drugs, but such was my sense of loneliness and despair that when a workmate offered me marijuana, I accepted it gladly. Over the coming months, I became a regular user, to the point where I would be real cranky and a pain to be around if I couldn't have any.

Having been born an only child and been a loner most of my life, I was shocked by how the loneliness was affecting me. I felt like I had a disease for which there was no cure.

I'd come to a point where God was quiet. I knew he was there, but I couldn't hear him. There were too many things in the way.

Melanie and I saw each other on a weekly basis, which seemed to keep the pain of it all at a high intensity. My Friday nights with her often ended with some sort of argument and we would part more as enemies than as friends. Friday nights would be followed by a weekend of deep depression.

I had purchased a knife which I carried around with me everywhere. It was a small pocket knife with a three-inch blade. I told myself that one day this would be the knife I would kill myself with. One particular weekend, I came to the point of deciding it was time to use it.

As usual, I had spent Friday evening out to dinner with Melanie. I think she only wanted to meet because she may have felt some responsibility to remain in contact with me until I went back to England. Or maybe, because I was still stupid enough to pay for everything! I never came away from spending time with her feeling anything but miserable. Why we did this every week only to end up arguing each time, I never really knew. I had come away suitably depressed and turned to my drugs and alcohol for solace, as I isolated myself in my bedroom. I was sitting on the edge of my bed considering my next move, when I remembered my knife. I walked over to the dressing table chair and took the knife out of the inside pocket of the jacket draped over it. I returned to my position on the edge of the bed. I pulled out the blade and pressed it into the inside of my arm just below the elbow joint with the intention of opening up my arm down to my wrist. Pressed hard against my skin I sat there just watching it. The skin was not broken yet, and wouldn't be until I moved the knife more purposefully. I just stared at it. And then a strange thing happened. It was as if my heart opened up and emptied itself of tears. I began crying as never before, in an uncontrollable way. As I cried, an amazing thing happened. It was as if God was leading me in prayer. I began talking to God in a way I had never done before, as my hurts, pains, and despair just began to pour out of my heart and mouth to God. I could articulate all my loneliness and despair into words I never knew I had, which God received. It was the unpacking of the burdens of my heart to the living God and I knew he understood. God was not condemning, judging, or giving me a hard time for the things he knew I had done wrong. God was listening. God was listening to the cry of a broken heart.

I'm not sure how long it went on for, but as I lay on my bed, I felt exhausted. I finished it with a simple prayer, "God, I want to kill myself, and the only reason I am not going to is because I know you don't want me to, but I don't know if I can stop myself. Please stop me as I can't stop myself. Thank you, amen." The next thing I knew it was morning.

I had had a breakthrough in my life with God, but the weekend was not over yet. The very next day, I was spiraling down into depression, and I thought about killing myself again. I remembered the knife and went to use it again, but I could not find it. I searched the whole room and could not find it. Strangely enough, by the time I had finished trying to find it I was so intrigued by the fact that I could not find it, that I had given up the idea of killing myself. The incredible thing was, that I would never see that knife again! I never discovered what happened to it, and I thank God for that. There was something else too, a big decision, I had decided not to continue to see Melanie. As it turns out, I have never seen her again since the choice was made. I could have seen her at Christmas, as she sent a letter saying something about it not being nice for me to be alone for Christmas. We arranged to meet in King George Square near the fountain. I did not keep the appointment. I figured, why flog a dead horse, it was time to move on even though the pain was still deep, and I missed not seeing her. It was a real lesson for me in learning to make choices that were best for me and my future, and not just making choices to please others. Looking back, it was strange really, to think that in the midst of my messy, painful, and disordered life, God was still with me. I had again begun to recognize the inner assurance and peace that I was actually where God wanted me to be.

Chapter 5

All, or Nothing . . .

I moved out of the hotel into a small one bedroom flat in Paddington. The place was furnished, and the bedroom was quite large, with a double and single bed, which both fitted in the room perfectly because of the 'L' shape of the room. A guy, named Tony, who I had met at the hotel, moved in with me and shared the rent. Tony was nine years older than me and had just gone through a divorce. There was a sense of consoling one another, but we generally lived separate lives. This worked fine for a few months, until he suddenly got fed up and left, and I was now alone with all the rent to pay. As I didn't know too many people, I did not really consider asking someone else to move in with me.

I was still struggling emotionally and coming to terms with all I was experiencing in my new-found life in Australia. There was also the question of my temporary Visa, which had now expired. In my usual way of dealing with most things, I just thought it would go away if I ignored it. It didn't. Out of the blue, I received a letter from Melanie, which had been forwarded to my new address. In it, she explained how she had been summoned to the Immigration Department and asked to give an account of the situation between herself and me. She told me how she had explained to the authorities that our not getting married was her choice and that there had been no intention on her part or mine to use the marriage visa to enter the country under false pretence. At least, Melanie didn't try to paint me as the bad guy in the whole thing, and I remember thinking it was kind of her to do that. The inevitable appointment with the Immigration Department arrived, and I was summoned to take my passport with me and give an account of what had transpired. It was just me and a guy behind his desk, in a small office.

Apart from the niceties, I only remember him asking me three questions. He seemed really embarrassed as he asked me, "Would you still marry Melanie if the situation was resolved?" I said an immediate "Yes," knowing it would take something of a miracle for that to happen. "Do you still have a full-time job?" I simply said, "I do."

"Would you like to remain in Australia?" I said, "I would like to." He asked for my passport, took it and opened it, pressed a rubber stamp on an inkpad and stamped my passport, closed my passport and gave it to me and said I could leave. That was it. I don't think he ever even looked me in the eye once.

As soon as I got out of the office, I opened my passport to see what he had stamped inside. It said, "Allowed to remain in Australia," and was dated from that day. I was genuinely happy, as I did really want to stay. Even though I had just been through some of the most emotionally and toughest months of my life, I felt at home in Australia. I just figured I was always meant to be here—and now I was allowed to stay indefinitely. I simply saw this as God's hand on my life. I was very optimistic about the future and what it could hold for me, but that did not last long.

Though overall I enjoyed living in Australia, it had by no means proven to deal with my more negative behavioural problems. Oh yes, to some degree, I had learned to stand on my own two feet with a job, a flat, and money in my pocket. But then I did my usual trick. I got depressed and left my job. It had been a good job; the one I'd been given in my first week in Australia, as a fitter and turner. Back in England, I had not finished my apprenticeship, but had done two years with a further four years of work experience in the trade. The company I had the job with was not a union place, so I didn't need the full trade qualification to work there. They liked my experience and gave me a go. All was fine for a while, until I allowed my personal problems to affect me yet again.

The longest job I had held, was my first job in England, which lasted for a little over two years. That ceased half way through my apprenticeship due to the steel industry in Sheffield virtually collapsing, together with England experiencing something of a recession. Since then, I could not hold a job down for very long. It was not the fault of the job, but mine. I was prone to depression, and I would get so emotionally down and feel such a deep inner pain that all I would want to do was die, so usually I left. After my first job, if I kept working at a job for six months, I thought I was doing well.

At this time at work, depression was getting a hold of me, and my thoughts were elsewhere, and not on my job. I would sometimes be turning a job on the lathe and be crying at the same time. Invariably, I made mistakes which made me even more depressed. Somewhat impulsively, I left the job. I just walked out one day and sent a letter the next day saying I was not coming back. I even suggested they keep any money owed me to pay for any mistakes I had made. Thankfully, a check for three-hundred dollars turned up for my final payment. This seemed like a small fortune, as normally, I only took home around a hundred dollars per week.

With meager savings, I battled on, wallowing in my despair. I knew the Lord was speaking to my heart, but I was trying to ignore him. But the day arrived when circumstances came to a head. I had little money, and was now three weeks behind on my rent and had no source of income. I was so low, the only food I had was a jar of peanut butter. Then the turning point came.

This particular day, the conviction in my heart was such that there was no escaping it. I tried to escape by going for a walk. The more I walked, the stronger the inner conviction became. All inside me seemed to be telling me to hand everything to God. I could not wait to return home; the conviction was so great. I just had to do something about it, but I had no idea what. Then it happened.

As I entered my flat, closing the door behind me, almost intuitively and out of my control, I fell to my knees and it seemed as if I slid a few meters to my bedroom. It was an "out of this world" sort of experience. I was suddenly on my knees in my bedroom looking up to heaven, with hands held high, reaching for God. I was desperate and literally screamed out to God, "OK, OK, you want my life? Well if you want it, here it is!" Amazingly, I then had the sheer audacity to add, "But before you take it, you can only have it if you take the lot. If you want the good parts, you have to take the bad parts as well or take nothing. That's the deal."

God's answer came instantly and clearly inside my heart, "I'll take the lot."

Immediately, my conviction was eased, and the Holy Spirit gave me inner peace with God, and I sensed my life was back on track. The point of change had arrived, and God did His work, "in the twinkling of an eye."

At this point, my circumstances had not changed, but I knew I had changed where it was important for me to change, on the inside. Suddenly, it seemed I had a fresh motivation, but nothing else, other than knowing, of course, that God was on my side. I signed on for unemployment benefits, and got an emergency check, which helped with the basics. A flat in my block became vacant, and the landlord asked if I'd decorate it for him. I did, and it solved my rent crisis. Then the note arrived. Pushed under the door was an urgent letter from the Employment Office telling me I was to go for a job interview the very next day. The position was for a Fitters Assistant with the Local Council Transport Department.

As I read the note, the Holy Spirit quickened me within to say the job was to be mine. I'd never experienced anything like this before, so I was very excited. I just knew this job was for me and I was going to get it!

There were at least eighty-two men who turned up for the job, as that was the number I counted that were sitting in the waiting area on the interview day. Well, eighty-three including myself. I was so certain the Holy Spirit was showing me that the job was going to be mine that as I sat, waiting for my turn to be interviewed, I was silently saying things to the lord like, "God it's not fair. You know the job is mine and all these people are waiting and being interviewed for a position they have no chance at securing." I even prayed for all the other applicants, that God would find them some other work, seeing that they had no chance at this job! I returned home waiting for the result of my interview, very confident in God that the job would be mine.

When I left the Transport Department nine years later to go to Bible College, it was the longest I had ever worked for one employer. All because I let go of the control of my life and let God take control. It was an amazing experience to know that the living God cared so much about my life. In my own small way, I felt so much in the will of God and somehow knew that his plan and purpose for my life was unfolding even further. No, I didn't have my life fully together, and I knew I still had life-controlling issues to deal with. But life was looking positive again, and I was surviving. After a few months of being a fitter's assistant, a position became available in the workshop stores section. Since I had briefly worked in a store before, I applied for the position and got it. I moved to another flat that was cheaper, and meant I could easily walk to work, once my employer relocated to the new premises being built in the Brisbane suburb of Toowong, which they planned to move to in just a few months. It worked out perfect for me.

Life was on the up.

Chapter 6

A Few Steps from the Brink

Although life was going well for me, I still did not go to church or pursue God in any significant way. As I understood it, Jesus was in my heart and I knew that when I died I would go to be with Him. That was still about the extent of my theology, really. Other than that, I just lived my life as I felt like it. I had no particular moral or ethical restraints, other than from time to time, God would speak to my heart. That had been a reality for me from the night I got to know Jesus. I had experienced His conviction and guidance and His ability to rescue me from life's circumstances. But still, I thought the Christian life was mainly about what happens after I died. I was genuinely looking forward to being with Jesus, one day.

I had no real Christian friends at this time, and simply partied with many of the people I had first met when living in the Kingsley Hotel. I mainly saw them on weekends, and we drank a lot. Back home in England, I mainly drank lager and only in halves, (half a pint) not pints, as I did not drink quickly, and a pint would go flat before I would finish it.

I've discovered that alcohol is seen in many ways, by various Christians. Some Christians call drinking a sin, and yet others embrace it. Some want it banned, and yet again others want it more readily accessible. It can help medicinally, to aid a person to regain strength after illness. For some, it can be resisted with ease; for others, it can drive them to the grave.

I never considered I had a problem with it. I'd grown up with alcohol in the home, from time to time. Throughout my childhood years, I was allowed a small glass of liquor or sparkling wine at Christmas time. Throughout the year, there were times when I would have a drink of beer, when my great uncle brought some home.

At around the age of fourteen, my mates and I would buy alcoholic cider and share it between us. We thought it was great. I really liked it, until the time when I was fifteen, and got drunk on it two nights in a row. After that, I could never drink it again. At age sixteen, I started going to the local disco and drank freely, underage. By the time I was eighteen, I drank regularly. Being legally allowed to drink, increased my consumption at various times, but I was not a big drinker. Mostly, I only had three or four drinks a night, which was all I could financially afford. On occasions, I would have much more, too much at times.

I would regularly, usually on weekends, go over my usual limit, and have been known to spend much time with my head down the toilet bowl as a consequence. I would even wake up with my head in vomit on the bathroom floor. The biggest mystery, was the night I decided to sleep it off by lying on a bench at the local sports field, only to wake up hours later halfway to the center of the field. I still think someone must have moved me.

When I drank too much, I usually alienated myself from friends. Not their fault, but mine. After heavy drinking, I always felt no one really cared about me, and would usually get very quiet, or take off by myself somewhere.

I never drank as much in quantity as some of my mates, but I did drink at every evening session at the Catholic Club that I could, plus Friday and Saturday nights at the disco, as well as Saturday and Sunday afternoons, when I had the chance.

When I arrived in Australia, aged twenty-two, I found the ice cold beer and style of pubs hard to get used to, but it didn't take long to adapt. Living by myself, I soon had the habit of having beer in the refrigerator, or alcohol of some kind around the flat. Beer was always an option for me, as Australian beer is more like the lager I was used to. With the depression I experienced through loneliness, I usually drowned my sorrows with ample amber fluid, as they called it. My drinking patterns began to change, where I would start drinking earlier, and finish drinking later, as time wore on. One blessing, (if you can call it that), was that when I drank too much, I never had a hangover, never. But one day, something happened to turn my drinking patterns around, and eventually made them virtually disappear. It was all down to the intervention of God in my life once again, with another "twinkling of an eye" moment.

What many people would never understand is, that by my having been born again, I had become a Christian and had been sealed with the Holy Spirit. This means that, where I had once been spiritually dead to God, I was now born again and spiritually alive to God. So even though my life was not perfect, God was still with me, by His Spirit living within me. So any time God thought it was the right time to speak to me, He would do so, by His Spirit within me. It's not an audible external voice for me, but an inner voice of the heart. And so, the time came when God had to talk to me about my drinking. And He did it in a very convincing way.

I'd had a few too many drinks the night before, and ended up sleeping in my lounge room on the couch. I woke up soon after sunrise, with the sun beginning to pour through my window, and the heat of the day beginning to fill the room. My mouth felt like it was lined with fur, and my first thought was that I needed a beer desperately. I had never woken up wanting a beer to start the day, but then I guess there's a first time for everything. From my vantage point on the couch, I could see the side of the refrigerator in the kitchen, and I began to make moves to get off the lounge. It was a hot and very humid Queensland morning, and as I was only wearing a pair of shorts, I had to peel myself from the vinyl couch. I focused my eyes on the refrigerator, and began to separate myself from the couch. It took some effort to get unstuck, so I sat up and rested. I then stood up, and started to walk toward the fridge that was about four meters away. I took a step forward, and then another, and then it happened. God spoke. As I went to take my next step, the Holy Spirit deep inside me said, "If you have a drink of beer now, you will become an alcoholic." I was instantly stunned. This was crazy. But immediately, I knew deep within, God was right. I'd never seen my drinking as a problem, but now in this briefest moment of time I could understand that it was. But I wanted a beer!!!!!! I just stood there virtually motionless not knowing what to do.

After a short while, I decided that moving any closer to the fridge was a bad idea. I returned to sit back down on the couch. For some reason, I felt really emotionally vulnerable and quite physically weak, and though feeling somewhat taken aback, I decided to pray. I told God how I now recognized my drinking was a problem. I told Him I really wanted a beer, and that I didn't think I could stop wanting it. I said if he was willing to change me, and stop me wanting it, then he had my permission, but I could not stop wanting it without his help. I asked him to go into the area of my heart that depended on alcohol, and to clean it out.

I didn't know what else to do, so I just laid back down on the lounge. I just lay there and snoozed, and sleepily pondered my life. By the time I got off the couch again, it was late morning, and I no longer wanted a beer. I can't recall when I next had a beer.

God had done something in my heart. Over the coming days, I realized that whatever it was that made me want to drink to excess, was now gone. The need for alcohol as a way of relaxing or having fun, or to block out pain, was no longer there as a need in my life. I did not stop drinking altogether at that point, but it was a turnaround. From that day on, I stopped regular drinking, and eventually arrived at a place where an occasional beer or glass of wine with a meal, is about my limit. Some years I may never have a beer, and I don't miss it at all. I also don't choose to drink in front of anyone I know who has a problem with alcohol. And I never drink if I will be driving.

I wouldn't really say I totally stopped drinking. I have to recognize in the Bible that Jesus turned water in to wine and that Timothy was encouraged to drink wine for his stomach because he was often sick. Jesus was even called a "wine bibber" indicating that he drank wine. Jesus also associated wine with the precious pouring out of his blood. God removed the desire within me to use alcohol in a negative way. Once the desire for what alcohol could supposedly provide was given into God's hands, he was free to do a work within me. And that is what God does, he transforms lives from the inside out, and very often, in the twinkling of an eye. But, alcohol was not the only drug I'd been having problems with. Marijuana was becoming an increasingly significant factor in my life. I no longer saw it as a real problem, because it fulfilled a need in my life to blot out pain, and run away, albeit temporarily, from my problems. Marijuana became my anesthetic, to cope with my reality. God would have to deal with that too. I just did not think he would do it so dramatically.

Chapter 7

Devil's Darkness to Light in Jesus

Whilst I was now experiencing more of the presence of God in my life, I still was not going to church. Even though I had now met a few Christians, I was not spending any significant time with any fellow believers. And to be honest, when it came to Christianity, my life was still pretty much a mess. I realize, looking back, that there were just so many things in my life that needed dealing with, but at the time I thought I was doing pretty well. After all, in general, my life was improving and was, as I saw it, on the up. I still simplistically figured I knew Jesus, and when I died, I would be with Him. While I keep repeating that same line of thought, it really was what I understood to be true, and was really the only truth I would cling to in time of need. I'd had no real Christian teaching, and still believed, thanks to The Children of God, that the mainline churches were not honoring God. It never really occurred to me that it could be at all possible that God had a real plan for my life in this world. But strangely enough, apart from my twinkling of an eye moments, I had a sense he was influencing my life more in some ways. As I think about it now, it is weird for me to see that, although God had proven himself in my life and circumstances, I was still too dumb to take it all in. I suppose, my walk with God was like my friendships with real people, where you see them a lot during periods and then you don't see them for a while. I was experiencing God in my life and it was good, but I was still merely drifting along in my journey with Him. I suppose, at the time, that's the way I thought it should be. My thinking on that matter was about to change dramatically.

Marijuana had become a significant part of my life by now. I would use it as often as I could get it. As I touched on previously, I had always said

I would never take drugs. In my thinking, drugs were the bottom of the barrel, and as low as a person could possibly get. So here I was, now smoking dope and loving it. Since I had been introduced to it by my friend from work, I had continued with it, in an effort to deal with my loneliness and depression during my first twelve months in Australia. For me, it was just an escape from the pain. Marijuana was just something to take my mind off my problems. It seemed to relax me, even if at times, I did not enjoy the experience.

The problem with my approach, was, that once I came out of my trip, the problems were still there. It was just a bit of pain relief really, and not a solution to the problems I was facing. God had dealt with the alcohol issue in my life, and that was an amazing experience for me. I did realize though, that I did not give up alcohol because of some theological teaching or because I thought it would make me a better person. I gave it up, only because God showed me it was a problem, and I gave the problem to him and he worked a miracle in me. I was somewhat the same with marijuana. At the time, I personally did not see marijuana as a problem. I enjoyed it. It filled a need. I wanted it. I had gone past the stage of thinking it made me a bad person. I took drugs, and I thought it was good, and I was cool. But God had different ideas.

I was not particularly looking to stop using marijuana. I actually thought it was fine and beneficial for me to smoke marijuana. I rationalized in my head that it was a naturally grown item, so maybe God wants us to use it. I also still smoked cigarettes at this time, which I had no problem with either. Anyway, I firmly believed that smoking pot was better than drinking too much alcohol. Even though I was holding a job down, I was late for work virtually every day, and pretty well depressed on all occasions, and that was why I figured I needed the pot; to be able to face myself and cope with each new day.

I would most often smoke pot by myself, as I found that the safest. This meant that on most nights, I had a joint or two. It was not hard to get hold of and was reasonably cheap. A deal would usually keep me going for a week or so. If I couldn't get hold of some, I would really get angry and on edge, and would not be a nice person to be around. I was not violent, but I would go into bouts of obscene language, or verbally attacking anyone who happened to be in my space. The guys at work knew what I could be like, and were known to dodge a low-flying bacon sandwich at times! I enjoyed my pot smoking. I had something of a ritual with it, smoking mainly in the evenings, just as it began to get dark and I always had some music on, in the background. Windows and doors were kept closed, except for the kitchen window, which was left open to clear the air in the flat. I always had a bottle of beer, so that, should anyone happen to come to the door while I was stoned, I could answer it with the bottle in hand and the smell of beer on my breath. That way, they might think I was drunk if I could not talk or stand properly. It is really quite bizarre to think about that the Lord had taken away my need for alcohol, and yet at this time I still kept some beer around to hide my drug taking. I preferred to lie on the floor, as it gave me less chance of falling over if I got fully stoned, and off my face. My experience of being stoned was generally fine, with insightful thoughts usually followed by lots of sleep. Occasionally though, I would go deeper into my depression, and would spend much time freaked out in the depth of loneliness and sad feelings.

Fortunately for me, God was beginning to have the habit of speaking to me when I least expected it. As I settled down on a balmy, Brisbane night to smoke a joint, I had no idea of the imminent move he was about to make.

I lay on the floor with my feet up on my couch, and lit my joint. As I began to drift into my trip, I felt quite at ease and peaceful. After a few moments though, I started to feel very uncomfortable. I no longer felt alone in the room. It felt like there was a presence there with me. The room started to go dark all by itself. It was weird, but I figured I could hold myself together, even though I thought it was going to be a bad trip. Then a voice spoke in the midst of the darkness saying, "I'm going to get you," in a sinister, and seemingly knowing manner. I began to freak out, as it seemed there was someone in the room whom I could not see, because of the darkness. It spoke again. "I'm going to get you." Instinctively I knew it was the Devil speaking. I could almost feel his breath in my ear. I had experienced virtually exactly the same thing the night I became a Christian. I generally don't mention this to unbelievers or young Christians when I share how I became a Christian. I would not want to discourage someone from making a decision for Jesus, because of fear of the Devil. The night I became a Christian, and I went back to my room, I had experienced the Devil's presence and those very same words, "I'm going to get you." This was along with a few other choice threats of how I would never survive as a Christian. It really scared me that first night, and it was only by talking to Jesus that the fear evaporated away and the Devil retreated. I knew nothing then of spiritual warfare and what it means for believers in their walk with Jesus.

Of course, growing up, I had heard about the Devil in the same way I had heard about Jesus. But by getting to know that Jesus was real by being born again, I learnt the Devil was real, and was now my enemy. Now and again, the evil one will still try to intimidate me.

So here I am on this particular evening, tripping out, and the Devil threatens me. I was totally freaked. I honestly felt I was in for something horrid that could not be stopped. I felt truly afraid, at a level I had never experienced before, as I now began to panic as the voice kept repeating its message over and over.

Then, the moment of realization came that maybe smoking dope was not what I should be doing, as a Christian. In the midst of my panic and fear, I cried out with the shortest prayer I have ever prayed, with the most heart I think I had ever put into a prayer up to that point. I simply screamed out, "Jesus!" In reality, that prayer was infinitely more than just one word, and I knew Jesus understood all that I implied in that shortest of prayers. That was it. My whole prayer, in one spoken word. Calling on the name of Jesus.

The answer to my prayer came as swiftly as I had prayed. The answer came in "the twinkling of an eye." The very moment I called on the name of Jesus, the darkness left the room and there was silence. Incredibly and amazingly, I instantly stopped tripping. That had never happened before. Instead of being enveloped in fear, I was now at peace in my heart and in my mind. All fear was gone. And here's the funny thing. A few moments beforehand, I was being freaked out by the Devil's intimidation. However, the way God answered my prayer *really* did freak me out more! Wow! What an experience of God working in my life again. Far above and beyond anything I could do myself. Amazing grace, and all in the twinkling of an eye! I knew nothing at the time about the Christian teaching of fearing God, but that night, I gained a realization that he is not to be taken lightly.

I was a new Christian who knew little, and was unsure of so many things spiritual. I had never been as scared in my life as that night, when the Devil threatened me, but that's all it was, a threat. When Jesus turned up to defend me, the Devil had no chance to carry out his threat. I've discovered that Satan wants to control us with fear, if he can. These days, I see fear as the opposite of faith. Jesus wants us to live by faith. Wonderfully, that night was the night of recognition that marijuana was a problem in my life that God wanted to deal with. That evening, through a time of prayer and confession, and repentance, my heart was renewed again. The desire for marijuana was removed, and I experienced another inner miracle, in the cleansing of my heart. My heart felt a bit like a house being renovated, one room at a time. Drugs were left behind in the light of a more powerful life influence, Jesus Christ as lord, now of that area of my life.

That night was a major turning point for me, in more ways than one. I realize anyone reading this will probably be wondering how I could not think that taking illegal drugs was wrong. But this was my journey, and my journey was just that, my journey. I learned a deep and wonderful truth. I learned Jesus does not condemn me at all, period. And that applies to all true believers in Jesus. No condemnation for those in Christ. I learned also that God fully accepts me exactly as I am, in Christ and will do all he can to bring about his best within me, and for my life. Yes, I was wrong to be taking illegal drugs. As a person, because the bigger problem was, they masked my real problems and stopped me facing up to the real issues in my life. As a Christian, they were wrong for me to take because I was putting trust and faith in something other than God. In the midst of all that I was doing wrong, God did not forsake me. When I turned to him he was there instantly with a big heart of acceptance and deliverance. Grace really is amazing. And all that was done yet again, in the twinkling of an eye.

The big lesson for me that night was that I learned afresh that God was absolutely serious about my life right now! Not just after I am dead and with Jesus. I now knew I needed to discover how to walk with God more purposefully. It was time to seek God anew.

Chapter 8

Jehovah's Witnesses

I knew I had Jesus in my heart, but now, I felt the need to follow God with all of that heart. God had shown me that this needed to happen through the miracles he had done on the inside of me. I was convinced now, that He was serious about my life and wanted to guide me in His ways. My work in the stores department meant that I very rarely saw anyone else except the guys I worked with. I was tucked away in a back corner next to a lift and every now and again someone would come down the lift to pick up parts I'd got ready for them. This all changed when the Transport Department moved to newly built premises. I ended up with a whole section, which meant that whilst still doing my normal storeman's work I now had a counter from which to serve. This provided more opportunity to meet guys from the workshops, and it was surprising how many Christians I would meet. I got to know quite a few, and we even occasionally spent some time together at lunchtime, talking about God and reading the Bible together. Also, some delivery men were Christians and would talk about Christianity with me. But, I was getting confused.

Nearly all the Christians I was talking to seemed to have a different view on what it meant to be a Christian, especially when discussing which church I should attend. I began to realize there were many Christian denominations, and as far as I could understand they all made their own rules for interpreting the Bible. They all seemed to think their doctrine and beliefs were the correct ones, even though they differed from that of other Christians. Each person I met from various denominations all firmly believed their particular way was right and others were wrong. One thing they all agreed on was that I should be going to church. But, they all seemed to think I should be going to theirs! So, which church to attend was now a confusing, but important decision for me to make. I seriously began to pray and evaluate which was the correct church to go to, and more importantly, the one God wanted me to attend.

A surprise answer to these questions came in the form of a Jehovah's Witness family.

One Sunday, on answering a knock on the front door of my flat, I opened it to find two people, a man and a woman, standing there. I guessed they were in their mid-forties and they turned out to be husband and wife, and Jehovah's Witnesses. I immediately wondered if maybe these people were God's answer to my prayers about which church I should attend, so I let them in.

They were very polite and friendly and acted as if they really cared about me. They listened to what I had to say and gave me positive feedback on any comments I made. They were very open to talking about God and always called him Jehovah. They showed me a small blue book entitled something like, "The Truth That Leads to Eternal Life". They suggested they could teach me God's truth from the book, by coming along on Sunday afternoons and spending around one hour together on a regular basis. I was eager to learn truth, so I agreed.

I knew that I knew Jesus, but that was about all. I did recall some childhood Bible stories that I really appreciated, but I had left most of that behind in my teenage years when I openly confessed I was an atheist. I knew nothing much, really, about Christianity, and as for any real Biblical truth was concerned, I was ignorant. But, I figured, maybe the Jehovah's Witnesses did know the truth, and if so, I would find out.

They began to come regularly, and each week we would go through a section of their little blue book, along with some verses from the Bible. After a while, they also sometimes brought their daughter along, who was around the same age as me. Her main reason for being there seemed to be to look into my eyes and smile at me a lot. The girl was attractive, so it was not hard to take.

The studies in the book seemed to be going well, but did not quite make sense for me. They seemed to have lots of "truths" that, for me didn't quite seem to fit together. But, who was I? I was ignorant, so what did I know? I kept going with the teaching as I thought it might start to make sense in the long-run, but over the weeks I became confused.

According to their teaching, on the one hand, Jesus was the Name above all names and yet on the other hand, there was no name greater than Jehovah. So, I figured logically, you can't have both.

God loved and accepted us in Christ, and yet if you became a Jehovah's Witness and sinned, you were thrown out. That didn't sit well with me.

They said heaven was for everyone, but only a 144,000 of the Jehovah's Witnesses would eventually go there, so that made me feel like I would miss out on heaven.

One week, between visits, I prayed to God as hard as I knew how about their teaching and if it was the real truth or not. I fell on my knees in my bedroom, and literally cried out to God something similar to: "Lord, I want to follow your truth. I don't want to be deceived. If the Jehovah's Witnesses are correct, please show me, but if they are wrong, please reveal it to me. I need you to speak to me; I can't work it all out, show me which way to go. In Jesus name, amen."

As I retired to bed that evening I had no idea of how the Lord was to answer my prayer but before morning my prayer was answered astoundingly.

I had a dream: I was standing in my bedroom in front of a wardrobe, with double doors and a full length mirror between the two doors. I was standing in front of the mirror with my arms by my side. As I looked in the mirror, something grabbed my arms and pulled them behind me and began to try to pull me down. I resisted. I couldn't see anyone else in the mirror, and I knew I must be being pulled down by invisible demons. As I was struggling not to be pulled down, I suddenly remembered what the Jehovah's Witnesses had taught me. They had told me that if ever I was in trouble, Jehovah was the name to call upon. So I began to call out to Jehovah but nothing changed, I was still being pulled down. I tried again, "Jehovah, Jehovah, in the name of Jehovah let go of me." And still nothing happened. It was not working as the Jehovah's Witnesses said it would. Then I called on the name of Jesus, "In the name of Jesus let me go." Immediately I was released and was able to stand upright again.

At the very next moment I experienced one of my most wonderful moments of my Christian life to that point.

I awoke, lying on my back, and immediately my mind was filled with the prayer that I had prayed before falling asleep, and the revelation that the dream was the answer to it. As if not in control of my actions, I sat bolt upright in bed and spontaneously began to praise and worship Jesus. God had answered my prayer. God had, as far as I was concerned, performed a miracle, and my heart just wanted to praise, worship and thank Him. Please understand that as someone who was not a church attendee yet, praise and worship as I experienced at that moment was still quite a foreign concept to me. Oh yes, I had sung hymns at school assemblies and at weddings, but to now worship Jesus from my heart like this, was wonderful and new to me.

I knew now, beyond any doubt, that Jesus was the name to call on and those who did would receive deliverance. The wonderful thing was that yet again, God had answered my prayers in the twinkling of an eye, even when my eyes were sleeping!

But now I had a problem. How would I tell the Jehovah's Witnesses not to come around anymore? After all, they had given me much of their time and were very good to me. Again, the lord provided wonderfully for me, but not before yet another urgent prayer, as they would be coming again on Sunday, in just a few days. It just so happened that on Saturday, the day before they came, I spent the day reading my Bible. In particular, I read the books of First Corinthians and Second Corinthians. On Sunday afternoon, there was a knock on the door. I knew it was them and I didn't answer the door. I stood with my back to the wall, next to the door, just wishing them to go away and never return without my having to face them. But deep down, I figured this approach may not work, as I guessed they would just keep returning week after week. There was no choice for me really, but to open the door. I prayed, "God, give me the words to speak, help me, in Jesus name, amen." I opened the door.

They moved forward as if to enter the house and I told them I didn't want them to come in. They smiled politely, and the man asked why. They were always so nice, it was very difficult to refuse them, and I had not planned what I would say, but just then, I remembered the readings from Corinthians and I gave them this answer. "In First Corinthians, Paul tells the Corinthians that the one who has committed a terrible sin must be sent out of the church. (They nodded in agreement) But in Second Corinthians, Paul asks the church to welcome the person back, so the Devil doesn't get the person. You don't do that. You told me that Jehovah's Witnesses accept people, but if they sin while they are a Jehovah's Witness, they are kicked out and never allowed to return." I stopped there.

To my amazement, they just said, "Thank you, Paul," and turned around and walked away. There was no argument, no trying to persuade me, and what's more, they never returned. God again had answered my prayer, by bringing those thoughts to my mind and giving me the words to say, and all yet again, in the twinkling of an eye.

I was now free from the Jehovah's Witnesses, with the heartfelt assurance and knowledge that God was guiding me. I had learned the important lesson, too, that Jesus was indeed the name above all names, and the one to call on in time of trouble. Any church I would be attending in the future, would have to praise and worship Jesus as lord. But first, there was the matter of what came out of my mouth on a day-to-day basis.

Chapter 9

Potty Mouth

M y mouth was foul. Even in my early teens, my friends would chastise me for my use of foul, vulgar language. It had come from my upbringing.

Being pregnant, and having nowhere to live, my mother had been taken in by her Uncle Colin and his wife Annie. Uncle Colin was one of my mother's uncles, and was one of thirteen siblings. Annie was his second wife and he, as far as I understand, was her second husband. He had no children by his first marriage, and Annie had at least four, that I later knew of. I'm not sure if her children still lived with her by the time she and Colin married.

I was a toddler when Aunty Annie died, but I still have a particularly fond memory of her. We lived in a two-story house. The downstairs had two rooms consisting of a kitchen and a front room, as we called them. Virtually, all of life happened in the kitchen. Front rooms were generally kept for special days and occasions. Aunty Annie's bed had been put in the front room, as she was a large lady, with poor health, and I guess probably could not climb the stairs to the bedroom. I remember her big smile when I used to dry and warm her bloomers. These were her underwear and I used to hold them high and wide in my hands in front of the kitchen fire, and then run into the front room where Aunty Annie was sitting in bed and ask her if they were dry or warm enough. She would always smile or laugh and say they weren't, which meant I had to keep running back and forth from the kitchen fire to Aunty Annie until the task was complete. I loved that. Sadly, my only other memory of her was seeing her in her coffin in the front room. The bed had been removed, and the coffin sat open on a table. People came to pay their last respects. I remember Mom lifting me up and telling me to touch Aunty Annie on the forehead, and saying if I didn't, I wouldn't be able to forget seeing her dead. I was a child, so I didn't understand what it was all about, but I touched her anyway. I've never forgotten her, dead or alive. Warming Aunty Annie's bloomers was one of my fondest childhood memories.

Sadly, when it comes to Uncle Colin, my memories are filled with sadness, deep pain, and regret.

It had been a sad life for Uncle Colin. He was my Great Uncle, and growing up I called him Uncle Colin. I know he cared about me in his own way, and I really believe he loved me, as I loved him. Sadly though, his life had a very detrimental effect on my upbringing. Uncle Colin was a veteran of World War One (WW1) and was mentally disabled, although you would not know it to look at him or to talk with him. He generally seemed fine, although I do recall that no one in the family seemed to have a good word to say about him. Though I do think they understood it was not just him, but his disability that made him the way he was. He used to speak of WW1 and especially of Gallipoli, Passchendaele and the Somme, amongst others. He had been shot in the lower leg, in the shin, and even fifty years later, I was able to put my finger in the bullet hole. But that was not his worst injury. He fought along with his brothers in the York and Lancaster Regiment, and one day in battle, there was an explosion and Uncle Colin was thrown into the air. He told me that as he was flying through the air, he passed another soldier and their eyes met. It was his brother Arthur. Uncle Arthur was injured from the blast, and I'm not sure of the extent of his injures. Uncle Colin said the explosion had "stretched his skull" and had given him damage in the head. I suppose he meant a head trauma that resulted in brain damage and mental health issues. Apparently, at one point, he used to have a lot of epileptic, or similar types of fits, and was even banned from the local Catholic Church for disrupting services there. I never saw him have an epileptic type of fit, but I sure saw him in fits of rage. It was frightening for me. By this time, Uncle Colin's sister, Elsie, Auntie Tess as I called her, had come to live with us to help look after Colin and myself, while my mom went out to work. Mom needed to work, as there was no financial support in those days for unmarried mothers. In fact, to be an unmarried mom was a terrible stigma and I always remember my mom being grateful that Uncle Colin took her in. I don't know what would have become of us otherwise.

You could always tell when one of Uncle Colin's fits of rage was coming, as there was a tension building in the house. For me, over time, it was as if the actual air got thicker and tried to smother me. It felt like the air would grab me around the throat and try to choke me. Auntie Tess and Mom would be getting stressed out, recognizing moment by moment Uncle Colin was becoming more and more agitated. As the expression goes, you could cut the air with a knife. Uncle Colin would be like a pot on the stove just simmering away and getting ready to boil. As I think about it, a boiling pot does not adequately explain what he was like, because he was more like a pressure cooker getting ready to explode. And explode he would!

All of a sudden, he would go off. It was not about anything in particular. He would just shout abuse at all of us, using the most vile and repulsive language you could ever imagine. In fact, most probably you could not imagine it—not without actually hearing it. It was obscenely disgusting. I had a regular diet of this language and abuse. I would cry and cry and cry and cry. He would say revolting things about my mother and I was helpless to do anything about it. Even though I was just a child, I felt responsible to look after my mom. It caused me to hate myself. Over time, I did learn to cope with it in my own way. I would just go over into the corner of the room with my pencils and paper and draw pictures or color. I would shut myself off in my own little world. I was alone and safe in my little corner. No one could hurt me there.

Hearing the foul words and abuse, taught me how to say things a child should never learn to say, and hence, as a teenager, it all started to pour out. In my own way, I became a mini-Uncle Colin. I was able to cuss and abuse with the best of them, and to be honest, better than the best of them.

It's really weird how we can rationalize and justify our behavior, when it suits us. As a Christian, I still swore wholeheartedly, with a firm conviction that should anyone say I shouldn't swear, then it was their problem. I was saved by grace, accepted just as I was by God, I knew Jesus and had the Holy Spirit in me, who was anyone to judge me! Well my times of foul-mouthed tirades were about to come to an end, by the hand of almighty God doing another inside miracle in my heart. And he did it, slap bang in the middle of my work day.

I enjoyed my job as a storeman with the Transport Department. I had been there a few years and knew my job well. Winter though, was the worst time to work in the lower store, where I was stationed. A cold breeze would blow between the stores counter and the open outside doors, in the

Reclamation Section just outside the wire-encased stores area at the end opposite to the counter.

Between the counter and Reclamation Section, was my desk. Needless to say, it was a freezing place to sit. I could not move my desk anywhere else, due to the shelving all around. But a brainwave was found. Someone had the idea that if a welding screen was borrowed from the workshop area and put in the front of my desk, I would be protected from the icy blast. The idea worked great, apart from just one thing. Normally, when I sat at my desk, I could see who came to the counter and often I could answer enquiries without leaving my chair. I liked this, as it meant less getting up and down for me, plus, the enquirer didn't need to ring the store's bell to get my attention, as they could see me.

With the screen in place, I started to become grumpy. The thing I hated most was serving a customer and then returning to my seat to be immediately disturbed again by the sound of the counter bell calling for my attention. And, of course, guys being guys, some would ring the bell as they walked past, and when I got up to look no one was there. I soon learned a great method of dealing with this issue. I would simply use excessively foul language at whoever pressed the bell, even before I saw who it was. If I was about to sit down and the bell rang again, I would pour out the abuse as I went to serve the "offending" customer. Now, the guys working in the workshop could handle this, no problem to them at all, but the workshop nurse was a different matter.

The nurse was a Christian, and had been trying to help me in my walk with the Lord. This particular day, I had just served a customer and was returning to my seat when the wonderful bell let out its marvelous chimes. I stood up in an immediate rage and opened my mouth to let forth a shower of abuse, when suddenly an amazing thing happened. It was as if someone had grabbed my tongue and had a grip on my heart at the same time. It just felt as if my heart was in the hold of someone's grip, as if being choked. And my tongue could not utter the words I wanted to say. It seemed nothing was allowed to come out of my heart or out of my mouth. It may sound silly, but I figured there must have been an angel standing there with me with one hand gripping my heart and the other stopping my tongue from moving. It felt just like my tongue was being held.

My mouth was silent. Not a sound would come out. I walked out from behind the welding screen and saw the nurse. I sighed a mighty sigh of relief. What if I had sworn at her? What if I had said something vulgar? My stomach turned as my heart remained in a vice like grip. I served the nurse and returned behind the screen. I made no attempt to sit down.

Without consideration if anyone else could see me, I bowed my forehead onto the top of the four door filing cabinet to the right of my desk. I prayed, "God, my mouth is sinful, it uses foul and vulgar language, and I can see now that the problem is in my heart. I confess my sin of swearing in my heart, and I ask that you would forgive me and cleanse my heart from this sin. Holy Spirit, come into this area of my heart where this sin lives, please clean it out, establish Jesus as lord of that area of my heart, and set me free. I ask this in the Name of Jesus, amen."

This happened nearly 40 years ago, and I can honestly say, I've never used foul language again since that prayer. As far as I am concerned, it was another miracle in my life, in the twinkling of an eye. I can't even say I had the will power to stop swearing. I take no credit for overcoming this issue in my life at all.

God set me free from a foul and vulgar mouth, or so it seemed, because I came to recognize that the real problem I'd had was a foul and vulgar heart. God went to the heart of the problem, brought deliverance and redemption, and glorified Jesus as lord of that area of my life. What an instant transformation!

I must admit, I was beginning to feel really blessed by God. All the ways God was changing my life were just totally amazing, even though I figured all Christians must have these types of experiences. But, God was becoming more and more real to me each day, and I was feeling close to Him. But now, He was about to take me through my deepest inner experience of him since the night I became a Christian. My understanding and experience of God was about to change significantly, and God would never be the same to me again.

Chapter 10

Father God

My dad was coming to see me. I was not school age yet, and used to ask a lot about where my dad was. The standard reply from my Mom was, that Dad was never home because he was a lorry driver, and was away working all the time. But, now he was coming to see me! I was filled with anticipation and excitement, because Dad was coming to visit. I'm not even sure how old I was, three, maybe four years of age, and for the first time I would meet my dad. Oh, it was beyond exciting. When the night came, in anticipation of his arrival, mom was making the kitchen tidy. The kitchen was the hub of the house, and life seemed to revolve around the big cast iron fireplace, which was the focal point of running the house. The fireplace was one large unit, comprising an open coal fire, a large oven, and a small oven above that. It had a large tiled hearth at its base, which stopped any hot ashes from getting on to the kitchen floor. Behind the open fire, was what we called, the boiler. This was the source of hot water for the household. It was very rare that the fire did not burn, even on the hottest of summer days, due to the constant need for hot water. In winter, the fire had to burn constantly so the water pipes would not freeze and burst. All cooking and baking was done in the fireplace. Above the fireplace, attached to rollers on the ceiling and controlled by a rope was the rack. This consisted of four strips of wood, each about six feet long, all slotted on either end into a cast iron coat hanger shaped frame. The rack could be lowered and washing hung on it and then raised high again so that the rising heat from the fire could do its job of drying. No washing on the rack tonight. Dad was coming.

My favorite place to sit was on the hearth, feeling the heat of the oven door on my back. As I sat there watching Mom, she seemed nervous as she was tidying the kitchen, even where it did not need tidying. All pots, pans, and dishes were put in the tall, built-in cupboard on the left-hand side of the fireplace. The kitchen table was cleared, except for two cups and saucers, milk and sugar. The teapot was warming in the small oven, with its door open, and the kettle sitting on the fire was already pouring out steam. Mom was tidying the couch that sat in front of the fire and was trying to fluff out the cushions, when suddenly, there was a knock on the door. I was so excited, because I knew it would be my dad. I had never knowingly met him, and I was sure it was not his fault he was away all the time. I figured my dad must be just as excited to see me as I was to see him.

As Mom answered the door, I positioned myself, standing between the fireplace and the couch, waiting eagerly to see Dad's face. He walked in, looking at me and smiling. I was the focus of his attention. I smiled too, but just stood there not really knowing what to do. I didn't have much experience meeting anyone's dad, especially my own. He reached into his overcoat pocket and pulled out a box of Liquorice Allsorts. Not the really big box I had seen at the green grocers, but the smaller yellow box that would have fit comfortably into his pocket. He reached out and gave me the box, which made it feel like Christmas to me. This was a special gift, and I tore the cellophane wrapper off the box as Mom mumbled something about saving them till later. Mom and Dad sat on the couch and I positioned myself in my favorite spot on the hearth. I strategically put the box of Allsorts behind my back for safe keeping.

For the first time in my life, I saw my mom and dad together. They just chatted away, and I remember my dad kept glancing down at me and smiling. In between glances, I would sneak an Allsort out of the box and into my mouth, and try to eat it without being caught. Dad may have seen me, but if he did, he said nothing. I'm not sure how long Dad was there. It seemed like one hour, but it could have been less. As he rose to leave, Mom motioned for me to stand up. I quickly jumped up as I was told, and forgot about the yellow box of Allsorts behind me. Mom asked me to pick up the box and offer an Allsort to Dad. I proceeded to do this with a cheeky grin on my face, because there were none left! I had managed to eat the lot without Mom or Dad realizing. It was a wonderful game to me. Mom was furious and started to voice her disappointment to me. But Dad was great. He gently asked her not to chastise me, and gave me a wink and another big smile as he made his way to the door. There was no goodbye kiss or special words; he just walked to the door. Here was my dad who I had just seen for the first time in my life about an hour ago, and now he was walking out of my life again. I just stood there, not really knowing what to do. A cold blast of winter air blew over me as Dad opened the door and walked out. I wanted to wave goodbye and see if I could see his lorry, so I ran to the doorway and looked out into the night. But all I could see was the black of night. It was as if dad and his lorry had vanished into the pitch black. He was no longer there. He was so close for a brief moment, and then gone. That dark emptiness took hold of me. I felt a sort of instant emptiness and coldness, as if darkness had just entered me. It would bury itself deep within me, waiting for the right moment to take me by surprise now and again.

Life moved on from that night and strangely enough I do seem to remember being a happy and somewhat content child, with a sunny disposition. I distinctly recall the sublime joy of laughing and making others laugh. It felt so good. I thought it was important to make others laugh. I can still manage to grasp something of the feeling of sheer joy it gave me to be able to run and express myself. I loved running, and would run anywhere I had to go, if I had the chance. Life seemed so big and wonderful to me. That was until "that day" came along. How I wish I had never known "that day". I suppose it was inevitable the day would come along sometime. But why when I was only five? Oh, I wish it had come at an age when I could have dealt with its implications better. The really sad thing for me was that from that day, I always felt I would be better off dead. That is not a pleasant feeling to carry around for more than forty years. Life can change so quickly. Even bad experiences can happen, in the twinkling of an eye. It only takes the briefest of moments for life-changing events to happen.

As far as I can remember, I was somewhat content in the idea that my dad was out there somewhere, and he would eventually come home to stay. It must have been around one to two years since I had met him, but I still knew one day he would return. The day that changed all that was a beautiful summer's day, when I was full of fun and joy, making my way home from school with two friends. Walking home from school, the three of us were having great fun. It was an instant adventure for us as Richard, Phillip, and I were walking home from what was known affectionately as, the "Sunshine School". The school was the only wooden house type building I knew of, and it was painted white. We were all in the same class, and often walked home together along Clifton's Snicket, which was a tarmac-sealed path, just a few feet wide and about 300 meters (three football fields) long that ran between house blocks from the school, past Clifton's grocery store and fish and chip shop, and connecting to Croft Road. Attempting to catch butterflies with our bare hands, was the order of the day, until we inadvertently ran into each other, and that turned into a boxing match. Philip and Richard decided to box first and I would be the referee. Each was to choose the name of a famous boxer. Philip went first and chose the name Billy Hawker who, at the time either was, or was close to being, the Heavy Weight Champion of England. I was glad he chose that name, as this was the same name as my dad, not that he was the boxer. I'd never let anyone know his name, so this was my big moment. As soon as Philip chose Billy Hawker, I said, "That's my dad's name." Philip didn't take much notice of what I said, and just gave me a glance, shrugged his shoulders, and took up his boxing stance in preparation for the big fight. Richard was different, and retorted immediately with, "That can't be your dad's name, because your last name is Cummings not Hawker. If that was your dad's name you would have the same one." I was stunned; devastated. I felt numb and my brain froze. In a daze, I processed what Richard had said. I had never realized or ever even thought of that. As Richard and Philip began to spar, I stood there in a trance. They were pretending to box and were calling out things, but I had no idea what they were really doing or saying. I was transfixed on what Richard had said, especially, "If that was your dad's name you would have the same one." Richard's words played over and over and around and around in my head; "You would have the same one, you would have the same one, you would have the same one." I felt dizzy on the words. They were spinning in my head. Around and around and around, I couldn't stop them. "If that was your dad's name you would have the same one." I felt like screaming, "STOP!" But I couldn't.

I knew I wanted to hide from Richard and Philip what I was experiencing. It was a strange feeling. I don't think I had ever tried to hide anything from anyone before, certainly nothing such as this. The boxing ceased, and we continued walking home, though I was in a daze and not really knowing what was being done or said. The implications of Richard's words were going over and over in my mind. My dad's name is different than mine. How do I know he is my dad? Are he and Mom married? Why is my mom's last name Cummings like mine, and not Hawker like my dad's? Has Mom been telling me lies? Have Uncle Colin and Auntie Tess been telling me lies? Do I have a dad? As we walked past the chip shop and on to Croft Road,

I continued in my head. Is Granddad my grandfather? Is Auntie Tess my aunty? As we reached the intersection of Croft Road and Coronation Road, Richard and Philip said their farewell and continued on, and I headed for home at Number One, Coronation Road. As it was the first gate up the hill, I did not have far to walk. I stopped walking and sat on the curb. I had to do some more thinking before I went in the house. Basically, it seemed my life up to now had been somewhat of a lie. My family had been lying to me and I was not quite who I thought I was. As I walked in the house, I could not look Uncle Colin or Auntie Tess in the face. I wasn't sure if I felt hurt, ashamed, betrayed, and abused or a collection of all of those, and more. For sure, I felt different now, as I immediately felt stripped of my generally happy disposition. I was wary, suspicious, and felt like I was not prepared to trust anyone. This all seemed to come on me between hearing of Richard's words and arriving home. It had been a twinkling of the eye moment. In one brief moment, my inner life was damaged in ways that would eventually, and often, take me to the pits of despair, and the point of suicide, and take many years to overcome. When Mom arrived home, I was different with her, too. I began to feel distant and separated on the inside. It took me a while to get to see the whole picture, but over the years, little by little, my mom unfolded the story to me.

I was born out of wedlock to Margaret Cummings and Billy Hawker. Mom and Billy had been childhood sweethearts, and intended to marry one day. At the age of twenty-one, my mom became pregnant at a time when society spurned such women, as well as children of illegitimate birth. As an older child, after I more fully understood my birthright, it was not uncommon for me to squirm whenever I heard the word, "bastard" spoken. It was not a name you called anyone in England, unless you wanted a fight. You could call someone every name and abusive term under the sun, but never call them a bastard. It was like signing a death warrant. The only term I knew used in the English language that was anywhere near as derisory was when strikers called their non-striking workmates "scabs". I realized over the years that being a bastard made me feel like a scab in society. It was a stigma I could not shake off. Being pregnant, Mom thought she and Billy would marry, but she had not figured on the attitude of Billy's mom. I think Billy's mom's name was Mary, and she and her husband ran a pub in Sheffield. It seems her husband was a bit of a weak character, and Billy's mom ruled the roost, so whatever she decided was final. Mom recounted to me how Billy's mom told her, "You are not one of us," meaning that Mom was not Catholic. So here is Mom pregnant and my Grandmother (I use the term loosely) instantly rejecting me. These two brief events in time defined my life for so many years. My destiny was shaped. I was born into a situation that was out of control, and seemingly without any real purpose. Mom had to find somewhere else to live. This led to my being born in, (or moved into just after my birth), a Christian place, that helped women in Mom's situation. Mom's mother had died when my mom was twelve, and so she lived with her father, who was her mother's second husband, and her two older half-brothers. I never knew Mom's dad, as he had always been in hospital, with what Mom described as a type of bone cancer. Mom never let me visit him, because she said his appearance would scare me. I wish I had met him. He died when I was around eight years old.

During the Second World War, Mom had to leave Sheffield, as many children did, because of the attempted bombing of the steel works. One of the places Mom moved to, was a village called Hoyland, around ten miles from Sheffield. This is where Mom got to live with Uncle Colin and his wife Annie, for the first time. That laid the foundation of Mom moving in there on the occasion of my birth, and with Mom no longer having anywhere to live, and needing to find somewhere urgently. Mom and I moved into One Coronation Road, Hoyland. As I mentioned earlier, Uncle Colin's and Aunty Annie's bed was in the middle of the front room, and I can never remember Aunty Annie being out of that bed. Most neighbors were pretty good to me and let me in their homes to watch television, or to give me an ice cube from their new and impressive refrigerator. One family's daughter even gave me my first forty-five (pop music record that is, not revolver!). It was a record by The Mudlarks called "Lollipop". It was a bit unusual because at the time, we didn't have a record player. Some neighbors were less kind and looked down on me, and at times, gave Mom dirty looks. Some didn't like their kids playing with me, but there was not much they could do about it. Then there was Mr. Fenton.

The Fenton's were our next door neighbors, who shared the same yard as us. Living in semi-detached council houses meant that you had your own front and back area, but you shared a common so-called front yard area. Both households entered the property through the same front gate. The Fenton's lived on the top side of the yard and had to use about seven steps to get to their front door. Living on the lower side we had just one step up to our front door. The funny thing was, that we all called our door the "front door", when in fact, it was the side door we were using. Living in the same yard with Mr. Fenton was difficult for me. He seemed a strange man. I would be playing by myself in the front yard and he would just stare at me. It just seemed sinister to me. He looked nastily towards me all the time. Something of what he was probably thinking was shown the day he, yet again, picked on me for kicking my football around the yard. I'm not really sure what he first said, but Uncle Colin came out and to confront him and it quickly turned nasty. I think Mr. Fenton was trying to get the last word, and threw a few insults about the family around, and then he pointed to me and said the words I have never forgotten, "And you can take that bastard back to Sheffield." Uncle Colin was about seventy years of age at the time and he ran from our front door up the Fenton's steps while Mr. and Mrs. Fenton were feverishly trying to get in their house and push the door closed. But Uncle Colin pushed against the door and forced his way into their home, and there was shouting and swearing, and Mrs. Fenton was screaming. I'm not sure what transpired inside their home that day, but from then on, Mr. Fenton stopped staring at me, and seemed to keep out of my way.

One of the hardest parts of having no father was the other kids. Not that they particularly picked on me because I had no father. Because of the lies I had been told, I had just naturally told those lies to others, as I knew no difference initially. The lies were the truth to me at first. Dad was a lorry driver and would be home one day. The thing was, once I knew the truth, I felt I could not keep telling the lie; yet, I just didn't feel I could tell anyone the real truth either. So, the hard part with the other kids was when they spoke about their dads. All perfectly natural for them, but for me it meant I could not join in the conversation and in fact, it meant I would withdraw when the conversation turned to the subject of dads. I just kept my head under the radar, hoping the conversation would soon change, and if it didn't, I would just walk away.

On arriving in Australia, I was less concerned by what people knew about my background. English people in Australia are often called Pommies. Australia was a penal colony for England, and some say the expression "Pommie" comes from the letters P.O.M.E on the original convict clothing, signifying Prisoner Of Mother England. Aussies also have the habit of calling Englishmen, Pommie Bastards just to see them get upset. When I was called a Pommie Bastard by Aussies, I used to stop them in their tracks. Normally, if an Englishman was called that in England it would most likely lead to a fight. The funny thing was, if Aussies called me that name I would just agree with them, and tell them they were correct. They never seemed to know how to handle that so I always felt I had one over them. They would either get very quiet or get very apologetic. I loved it!

Because I had learned to cope with being illegitimate and was now in my mid-twenties, I had no idea that the matter of fatherhood was something God wanted to begin dealing with in my life. He did it in a way at which I still marvel, and am still so thankful for, these many years later.

On becoming a Christian, having never really known what it meant to have a father, I really wrestled and struggled with the biblical concept of God as my father. Although I had read and heard it, I was not able to apply that truth to my life in any significant way. I could still only call him God and was not able to address him as father. I wanted to believe that he was my father, but something inside seemed to stop me being able to digest it fully. In my head, I believed it, but to my heart, the idea seemed foreign. In my prayers I could not call him father, only God. I didn't see this as a big issue for me, and it wasn't as if I was thinking too much about it, but God had another idea.

I still wasn't attending a church, but I was spending more time with the Christians at work. Mainly, there were six of us who would get together outside of work hours to spend time together around the Bible. Along with myself, there was the nurse, two guys from the Electrical Section, who had just recently become Christians, and their wives.

Here's the amazing thing. I believed God was telling me to get together with the five of them. I still can hardly believe that I went to the nurse and the two guys and said that God wanted us to get together for a specific meeting. They asked me why. I said I had no specific idea why, other than the lord has something I have to say. I really was flying blind, so I just reinforced that God wanted us to get together and that was all I really knew. Looking back it sounds crazy, but it's what actually happened. So, we arranged a time to get together at the nurse's home one evening. It felt strange asking people to come together without giving them a reason, but it also felt so right.

On the night of the meeting, we all greeted one another warmly and sat in the lounge room and chatted. The meeting was going nowhere in particular, which was fair enough, as there was no agenda other than to come together and meet and God would somehow speak to us. We continued chatting until one of the guys nervously asked me, "Why are we here?"

I had no answer in my head, but I opened my mouth to try and explain that I was not sure why, but that I believed God was going to show us why. I never got the words out. As I opened my mouth to speak, I burst into tears. From absolutely nowhere, I began to cry helplessly.

They gathered around in support, and I remember laying my head on someone's lap as I continued softly sobbing. They began to ask me questions and, this part was truly amazing, because every question they asked it was as if God was asking it! It was their voices, but God was in control of them. God was speaking directly to me through them, and straight into my heart. As my head was buried in someone's lap, and I was either sobbing or at times wailing away, I wasn't looking at faces or surroundings. I was only hearing voices, and while I knew it was these people, it was also true and very real to me that God was speaking to me.

It was as if Jesus, through them, was asking me the questions I needed the answers to. It came to focus on questions about my lack of a father, and how that had affected my life. Each question took time to answer between tears, but each answer drew long standing pain from the deep well of my heart, and every time I answered, I felt sort of better. Over a period of an hour or so, I poured out my grief of having never known a father. Whenever I poured out more grief, it was as if God comforted and healed me in that particular area and gave me a sense of peace inside. This became more apparent in the days following, but right there in that lounge room, I poured out my loss of a father, and was led to acknowledge and receive the truth that God is my father. I learned that whatever this life may rob us of, God can restore, for He knows our every need, no matter how deep down it may be.

I was the humblest and happiest man in the world, as I said goodnight to my friends. God had performed another "inside miracle," in the twinkling of an eye and my life would not be the same again. And I didn't even know I needed it. But, there was a more wonderful joy to behold.

As I retired to bed that evening, I read my Bible and said my prayers as usual, but now I noticed something different. As I prayed I said, "Dear Father," and as I said it I was struck with the thought that before then I had only prayed and said, "Dear God." He was still God, but to me now, he was much more than God, he was a father. I love you, my heavenly Dad.

Chapter 11

Audio Visual

There are things in our life that can be a distraction to following God. For me at this time, the main distractions were my television and the music I bought and listened to.

Living alone, I found that television was a great comfort for me. I had a little color TV that I rented on a two-year contract, which would be terminated in a few weeks' time. I had never once thought about not renewing the contract, but as the time drew nearer, I was experiencing a conviction from God. It was not that God was showing me that TV was a wicked, evil thing, but more a case of the time that I spent watching TV could be put to better use. I began to see that there was rubbish on TV that was not edifying and uplifting for a Christian. Some programs were downright bad and useless for a Christian, and yet I still watched many of them. Habits can be difficult to break, and especially so when one's comfort is attached to them. I was feeling nervous to say the least, but figured I could give up TV for God, if he gave me the strength. The day came, and the TV was taken away. I just stared at the empty space for a while. The timing of God was impeccable. My first weekend without the TV was the same weekend I had had to say farewell to the Jehovah's Witnesses, so, having no TV meant that I turned to the Bible to pass my time. I read First and Second Corinthians (I would normally never read so much), and it was there that the Lord had given me my answer to the Jehovah's Witnesses when they came knocking at my door. It reinforced for me the immediate benefit, and potential future benefits, of being without a TV.

Around this time, the Lord also dealt with another media issue that had a strong grip on my life, music.

Living in my little flat, I still went through times of feeling very down, because of being alone. I had made friends in the two years I had been in Australia, but I was a changing person now. The friends I had made were in a different place than me, as their values were different than mine. I was being changed into a new person—the one God wanted me to be. Not that I felt better than them, or that I wanted nothing to do with them, it was just that my values were changing in a Christian direction and that was not the case for my friends. I grew up hearing the expression, "God moves in mysterious ways," and that was surely happening in my life at this time. My music now seemed to be an increasing issue of scrutiny by God.

Before I left England, I had copied a lot of my singles on to cassettes. I was only into popular music, and had quite a broad range of what I liked from ballads, to blues, and rock-and-roll. I'd added other bands and singers to my collection, since my arrival such as, heavy metal and punk bands, like Led Zeppelin, and the Sex Pistols, but even the more ballad style of Simon and Garfunkel, and Jim Reeves, found their way into my music collection. The thing with my music was that when I listened to it, I got depressed. I could listen to the Sex Pistols and enjoy the raw energy, but the lyrics were excessively negative for me. Surprisingly, the worst for me were Simon and Garfunkel. Even though their music had some lovely melodies and words, I would sometimes feel suicidal after listening to them. I'm in no way saying all music is bad, just that at this time, I was beginning to recognize how bad my choice of music was for me. I didn't realize it at first, but what was in fact happening, was that the Lord was starting to show me how negatively influenced I was by the music I chose. I depended on it for emotional support, and yet it did very little to support me. When I was home, I would have music on virtually all the time. It went around and around in my head and heart. The lyrics, to varying degrees, would guide my life and my values. I think this was an issue for God who is a loving, caring, and jealous God, and only wants the best for His children. He wanted the best for me and didn't want my thoughts and heart to be taken away from Him. Needless to say, I was not of the same mind. Playing my music became increasingly difficult. I would wrestle with God to play it, and then when I did play it, I would get depressed. I did not want to let go of it, but the thing was that I had begun to ask God to guide my life and show me His will. I had now come to the place where I really wanted to be the person God wanted me to be, and to do the things God wanted me to do. I was beginning to realize that God takes such prayers seriously, and that the truly wonderful thing about such prayers is that it allows God the freedom to work in our lives. It's as if God is just waiting for our permission for him to change us. Never once have I felt God bully me or try to violate my free will. He has never even once used condemnation as a tool to challenge me to change. But He has got alongside me and asked me why I do certain things, and encouraged me to commit my ways to Him. The music issue was a particularly difficult one for me though. It came to the point where I so did not want to let go of my music, and yet I became so convicted that I was shouting at God. All I had was a cassette player that had two detachable speakers on wires and a handle across the top of it. I was screaming and shouting at God that I did not want to let go of my music! Then I broke. That still small voice of God finally got through. I grabbed the handle to the player and threw the whole lot across the lounge room as I screamed at God, "Here it is, take it, take it, you can have it!" The cassette player smashed into the wall and onto the floor. I felt an instant relief. I had fought, but God had won. I don't even know if the cassette player still worked. I picked it up and put it in the garbage bin. I got rid of all my cassettes and was left with no music at all. Strangely enough, I felt great.

Without the negative influences of TV and music, I was now set free to pursue God with less distraction. There was another spin off from this too, as I started arranging my day differently, and even going to bed early, because I no longer watched TV till late.

I hated getting up early for anything, especially work. It was always difficult for me to get out of bed early in a morning. Time keeping was definitely not my best attribute. From my early days at my first job, I struggled to get to work on time. Maybe only a few minutes late, but late all the same. I tried my best with my first job but after that became history, I went downhill rapidly.

I could be anything up to an hour late for work and if I thought I would be too late, I just wouldn't bother to turn up. This was not easy when I lived at home, as Aunty Tess would always try to wake me up, but when I moved to Australia, it was a different story.

If I was depressed, I wouldn't go to work. Once, I was depressed for a week and never called work, so days later I had to visit a doctor for a certificate to cover me. He had no right to provide one, but he did. If it was raining and I might get wet, I wouldn't go to work. It got to the point where, if there was a big day ahead at work and it was raining, my boss would send a truck to pick me up, as he knew I wouldn't turn up otherwise. My time keeping became so bad, that I would be up to three hours a day late for work. My boss covered for me, and I suppose as no one ever said anything to me, I got away with it. Needless to say, I was becoming convicted by the Lord that this type of behavior was not appropriate for one of God's kids.

I don't recall any wonderful move of God over my life about this issue, except to say that the Lord gave me a simple choice; either continue on as I was and live with the future consequences, or get to work early. I figured there was something I should take notice of in the "future consequences" bit, so I prayed that the Lord would help me to succeed with this. Strangely enough, after I made the conscious decision in God to be early for work, God did a new work in my heart and mind.

Agreeing with God helped me. My old attitude changed, and I could now see the importance of good timekeeping. I realized good time keeping is a part of loving others. It lets others know you care enough about them to be there on time. It stops others having to worry if you are okay, or if your late arrival possibly means you've had an accident. It means others can make alternative arrangements, based on your caring enough to contact them if you are to be late, or are not going to turn up at all. Yes, the Lord showed me, to be punctual was actually caring and loving. Agreeing with God on this issue, brought a change in my life that was wonderful.

I lived close to a bus route which had few buses, but three very good ones for me. I had no clock in my flat, so I now started naturally arising from bed at sunrise. The first bus of the day would go past my flat at 6:30 am, by which time, I'd been up, had my breakfast and shower, and would have everything ready to go to work. So, this first bus signaled it was time to read my Bible until the next bus at 6:55 am. Then, I would leave for work, to which I could walk in about 15 minutes, arrive early, have a cup of tea and begin my working day in a relaxing way. When I came home from work, I would relax at home in the evening until the last bus at night went past at 9:25 pm and that told me it was bedtime.

From being hopelessly late for work, I was now a new person, arriving fresh and on time. But the really amazing thing for me was this: on the very day that I agreed with the Lord to be punctual for work—on the very day God changed this area of my life, my boss came to me and said; "Paul, I can't cover for your late attendance anymore." I just said, "It's okay: the Lord has sorted it all out, and I won't be late anymore." He raised his eyebrows, shook his head in disbelief and walked away. I was never late again.

Much later, a funny thing did happen though. I was in bed one day, and did not want to get up for work. I stayed in bed after my rising time and wanted to stay there. The conversation with the Lord went something like this;

"Paul, it's time to get up."

"I know."

"You'll be late for work."

"I'm not going to work."

"Come on, Paul, get up for work."

"I'm not going to work."

"Are you sick?"

"No."

"Come on, get up for work."

"I'm not going."

"You'll be late, if you don't get up now."

"I'm not going today."

"Come on, Paul, get up for work."

"No."

"Are you sick?"

"No."

"Come on then, get up for work."

"No I'm not going."

"Paul, get up for work."

"No."

The lord stopped talking, and there was silence. If there is one thing I have noticed about the silence of God, it's this; it's *deafening*! Within around five minutes, I was out of bed, dressed and off to work. I seem to remember doing a lot of apologizing to God on the way to work that day.

When God changes our lives, he wants us to stick with it. The TV and music issues in my life were not dealt with as dramatically as some other things. The journey to freedom from their control however, still brought some twinkling of an eye moments as God did his masterful works of deliverance and restoration. With those things no longer dominating my life, I was able to put my time to better use, and bring discipline within, more fully. Today, I again listen to music and have a TV, and enjoy both, but the difference now is, that I don't need them, and am able to discern what is good, bad, or indifferent about them. To be honest, while there are occasionally some things worthwhile to watch, I find TV is primarily broadcasting unhelpful rubbish, which I don't watch. Music can be better, but so much of it is negative, that I don't entertain it much, other than selected Christian music. I find that I prefer silence and solitude, as I can hear God better that way.

Chapter 12

You Don't Smoke Anymore

John was a seventy-year-old retired Dutch gentleman who was a true brother in Christ, and a great support to me. He had moved into the flat next to me, just a few weeks before I moved out. I'm not sure how long he had been in Australia, but I found his accent quite difficult to understand. He used to talk of Sheen Shallenge, which I had never heard of and which turned out to be Teen Challenge—which I had still never heard of!

John was attending a non-denominational church called Jubilee Fellowship, which had developed out of Teen Challenge, mainly to support people dealing with, and getting free from, addictions and life-controlling problems. The mainline churches often found new converts from the drug and street scene difficult to assimilate into their churches, due to the massive clash of values. John invited me to attend the church, as he knew I was not going to one, and believed I should be. It met on Sunday afternoons at 3.00 p.m. for an hour of teaching, input, and then after a short break, there would be an hour long worship service—and then downstairs into the hall under the church for refreshments. I don't remember much about the teaching or the worship service, but I do distinctively remember the time in the hall. Although I was having fellowship with some Christians at work, I was really taken aback by the Christians I was having refreshments with. The striking feature was that they seemed so loving. I was really aware that there was love in that room, and that it radiated from the people there. They readily accepted me, and seemed to be genuinely interested in me, and were like a breath of fresh air into my life, and I found it wonderful. The Christians at work seemed to be more concerned about various doctrines, and making sure their teaching was correct. Though that was important, I could now sense that love was the one thing that really mattered.

Because of my immaturity as a Christian, I allowed my work friends to discourage me from attending Jubilee Fellowship again. They spoke of it as something to be very wary of. I thought they possibly knew best, and left it at that, but I could not forget the love I had experienced at Jubilee, and it was to become an important healing component in my life in a significant way.

I moved out of the flat next to John, and spent much more time with the Christians at work, not only at work, but at other times, as well. After a few months, I was finding the lord speaking to me with his gentle voice in my heart. I had the sense He was saying something along the lines of, "I have given to you, now go and give to others." I was not fully sure how to live this out, so I shared it with my group of Christians. Boy oh boy, did that bring a response. They were quite blunt in their reaction and told me in no uncertain terms that if I went off to do "good works" as they called it, then I was trying to earn my salvation and not trusting in the cross of Jesus. They summed it up quite succinctly by telling me I would blaspheme the Holy Spirit.

I was devastated. That was the only sin in the Bible that could not be forgiven and they were saying I was about to commit it. I felt lost. At the time, I was living in the house of one of the group members, so I very quickly found a flat and moved out.

Though I was struggling with the accusation, I knew God was active in my life and deep down I knew it was his will that I go and help others in some way. I knew I was not trying to gain salvation by going out to do good things rather than trusting in the finished work of Jesus on the cross. Even so, I found it really difficult to pray and found my main prayer life consisting of reciting over and over the Lord's Prayer. I also took solace in the scripture that said: " Therefore I want you to know that no one who is speaking by the Spirit of God says, 'Jesus be cursed,' and no one can say, 'Jesus is Lord,' except by the Holy Spirit." (I Cor. 12:3 NIV)

Satan was really attacking my mind, and trying to tell me constantly that I was finished. Every night, I would go to sleep reciting over and over and over that Jesus Christ is Lord. I knew I could not really say that and believe it, unless the Holy Spirit was with me. It was a torrid time in my spiritual journey. It was at this point that I remembered John and Jubilee Fellowship.

John looked at me very suspiciously as he opened the door. I could tell he knew something was wrong, but he let me in and we just chatted about general things. I said I would like to go to Jubilee Fellowship again, and he was very open to that. We went together the very next Sunday. Though it was not a mainline church, it ended up being the first church I attended on a regular basis, as a Christian. I did not share too much about what had happened to me, but I attended the church and one of the church's home groups, regularly. For some reason, even though church was a new experience to me, I believed I should attend every week. It was the highlight of my week.

Over time, I got over the accusations of my work colleague Christians, and even went to visit them all at a gathering they were having one Christmas. They still tried to tell me I was wrong, but I just decided to try to love and accept them and not argue. A couple of them were really impressed that I had visited and challenged the others to listen to me. I didn't go there to tell them I was right. The reality was, that for a time the Lord had used them in my life for my benefit and I was truly thankful for that. I was even thankful now, that I had gone through the torment of their accusation, as I knew I was now a stronger Christian because of it.

Most of the members of Jubilee were involved with Teen Challenge in one way or another, and when one of them stood up in church to ask if anyone could volunteer at the Teen Challenge youth shelter called "Hebron House", I knew that was where the Lord wanted me to serve. I became a volunteer there on a regular basis.

John and I would meet together at different times for fellowship and prayer, sometimes at his flat and other times, at mine. One night at my place, John asked for a specific prayer so he could stop smoking. He had a real hang-up about his smoking habit, and he felt constantly guilty, because he wanted to stop and couldn't.

I found this a bit of a pain, as I spent much time with John and I also smoked, but I didn't see it as a problem. I was smoking up to three packs a day, and could not afford to continue doing so. To save money, I started to buy tobacco and cigarette papers and roll my own, but now I was going through a pouch of tobacco a day. Even so, I saw no real reason to stop smoking, except for John telling me it was wrong.

Even when we didn't meet primarily for prayer, whenever we spent time together, we would pray before going our separate ways, and John always insisted we pray for each other to stop smoking. I cooperated, but only to humor John, and try to support his desire to change. So, this evening in my flat seemed no different from any other, as we concluded our time together as usual, in prayer to stop smoking. At times, smoking had become a bit of a ritual, and one such ritual was, that I would always roll a cigarette to smoke while driving John home. So, naturally as I would be driving John home, I rolled my ritual cigarette for the journey. We got in the car and as I sat in the driver's seat, I put the cigarette in my mouth and went to light it, but before I had time to light it, the Holy Spirit spoke to me inside saying, "You don't smoke anymore."

It may sound odd or strange to say this about an inner "voice", but it was so clear that I thought John could have heard it too. I glanced at him to see if he had heard anything, but he was oblivious to what was happening to me. I didn't want to say anything to him.

Within myself I just said, "Oh yeah, sure Lord," and put the cigarette in the ashtray for later. (I didn't realize it at the time, but this was another twinkling of an eye moment)

I dropped John at home and, as my usual habit was to have a smoke on the way home, I picked up the cigarette, put it in my mouth and went to light it. Again the voice said, "You don't smoke anymore." My response this time was to laugh to myself and say, "Well Lord, I won't light it up, but I know and you know, I'll need it soon." I arrived home without lighting the cigarette, and carried it into the flat with me. The last thing I would do before getting into bed each night, was to have a smoke, so again, I picked it up and yet again the voice said, "You don't smoke anymore." I went to sleep.

At 6:00 am, the alarm woke me as usual, (I was in a different flat now and had no buses to keep time for me), and I reached for my starter smoke for the day, and again the voice was there—waiting: it said, "You don't smoke anymore." I was too tired to respond, and just put the cigarette down and went for a shower, and had breakfast and left for work.

Of course, I pulled out the ciggy again to smoke on the journey, but again the voice inside said, "You don't smoke anymore." The same thing happened when I arrived at work; all my usual smoking routine was thrown into disarray with the seemingly perpetual voice, saying "You don't smoke anymore."

I honestly didn't think that I had permanently stopped smoking yet. I'd even say to the lord, "Yeah, sure Lord, I've stopped smoking for now, but I expect in the near future, I will light up again."

For this reason, I continued to carry my tobacco packet around at work and at home for three days. Every time I went to smoke the same cigarette, the voice would say, "You don't smoke anymore." Eventually, after three days, I pulled the tobacco and lighter out of my top pocket and dropped them into the garbage bin whilst saying to the Lord, "You're right Lord, I don't smoke anymore." I never smoked again. My smoking habit was gone and I couldn't take any of the credit, praise God.

But the story didn't end just there. Along with the victory came a simple yet effective temptation. Will, my boss, would sometimes have a cigar for me, which he often received at weddings or special occasions. I had not yet told anyone that I had stopped smoking, and he gave me a large Winston Churchill type cigar, on a visit to his office. I took it down to my section of the store, goggle-eyed in eager anticipation of devouring it. I told myself a cigar was not like cigarettes, it's different; it's on a different level, not real smoking. I moved the cigar to my lips but before it reached them, guess what I heard? "You don't smoke anymore."

I took the cigar to Will's office, put it on his desk, thanked him for it and said, "I don't smoke anymore." He fell into his chair in utter amazement, and the chair rolled backwards, into the wall behind him. But, now I had confessed the victory, there would be no going back.

I can never truly take credit for having stopped smoking, because it was something the Lord did for me. I like it when all I can do is say, God did something in me or for me, and it was not my own strength or will power that achieved an end result.

Probably, the only sad thing about the whole experience was that poor old John, as long as I knew him, never stopped smoking. Poor guy, he felt so guilty. Still, his prayer was answered; my smoking stopped.

Chapter 13

Getting a Wife

After a while, I moved in to a flat with John, and another guy named Dan, who, I guess was in his mid to late fifties. Six months later, I was approached to see if I would be open to living in a Christian singles house. There would be five of us, all mainly with a background of involvement in Teen Challenge. I was open to the idea, and after a meeting of the five in my bedroom, we decided to find a place to rent.

It took a while, but we ended up renting a five-bedroom house on Miskin Street in Toowong, Brisbane. At the time, we simply referred to it as "Miskin Street", and even years later the name elicits many various memories.

The initial five were, Warren, June, Sue, Christine, and myself. Sue left soon after moving in, and Tracey took her place. We would have a weekly, Monday night meeting to clear the air on any issues, and to set the rules of the house. We came from various backgrounds, so that was a bit of a challenge, which we met full on by listening to one another, and taking a vote to decide the majority way forward. The five of us stayed together for around 12 months before there were any changes, and it really was a positive experience overall. Yes, we had ups and downs, but we worked through them and bonds of Christian love and friendship grew. From my perspective, it was a time of personal growth, and I'm sure it was for the others too.

My main problem was that I liked my privacy, and did not really want to share personal things. This was especially true if it came to any possible romantic relationships I may have been exploring. The cat was out of the bag though. June had discovered I was taking a friend of hers out for dinner on the coming Friday, and somehow Christine found out about it too. I did not want anyone else to know about it.

A day or so before my dinner date, we were gathered around the dining room table having dinner together. Our aim as a household was to have dinner together on week nights. Each person had a night of the week to cook. This particular night, we were chatting away around the table, and Christine chirps up and asks me in front of everyone, "What are you doing on Friday night." Unbeknown to me, Christine had totally forgotten I was taking someone out to dinner. Of course, I did not realize this, and I thought she was trying to embarrass me into an answer. She kept asking, and I kept refusing to answer until eventually I blew my top and stormed out of the dining room, after nearly tipping the table over. I was so freaked out about anyone knowing I was going on a date. It was just the "date thing" that bothered me. I had lots of women friends who I would go off for the day with sometimes and just have a friendly day out. That was just normal friendships, and I didn't care who knew about such times. But, when it came to taking someone out on a date, I just wanted it to be kept secret. Maybe my past rejection with Melanie was still affecting me psychologically, without me really understanding it. Needless to say, when I took a girl on a date and they did not want to go out again, it would always hurt me. The funny thing was, even if I knew I didn't want the relationship to go any further, it still hurt me.

It was a bit of a touchy subject for me, as I was now hitting my late twenties and heading for thirty, and had started to ask the Lord for a wife. I didn't set any particular expectations, other than that she had to be a Christian who was committed to, and loved Jesus. I just left it at that really. I'm not sure how many times I prayed for a wife, but the answer to my prayer, or at least a part of the answer, came quite quickly and unexpectedly.

One evening, when settling down into bed, the Lord spoke to me. It went like this:

"Paul, get out of bed, and bow down before me. I have a message for you."

"Oh lord, I'm in bed. Can't you just tell me while I lay here?,"

"I want you to get out of bed, and bow down before me. I have a message for you."

I will admit to feeling somewhat inconvenienced, but I proceeded to get out of bed, and kneel on the ground. I bowed down my head to the ground, with my arms outstretched to the lord. He said, "I am going to send you your wife. But you have to be careful, or you may miss her."

Silence. That was it. I thanked the lord and went back to bed.

From that moment on, every woman I met, I would ask the lord; "Is this the one?" After all, I had to be careful I did not miss the person the Lord was sending. I met lots of ladies who I knew nothing in particular about, and who were not women I would normally think of asking out. But what did I know? I just had to try to make sure I did not miss the one the lord was sending to be my wife.

Strangely enough, around this time there was a lot of tension in the house because of myself and Christine. Whenever we had one of our house meetings, Christine would always be questioning me, and want to work out why I thought the way I did. We basically fought a lot. Not nastily, but just agreeing to disagree, and at times being quite frustrated with one another. It did come to the point though, where I was beginning to suspect Christine was liking me more than she should, and maybe that she was even attracted to me. I'm not sure what it was really, just a sense I had. I did not want to encourage this because, firstly, I didn't really want to get romantically in-volved with her. Secondly, our house rule was that there were no romantic relationships between members of the household. I went to see my mate Mick, and told him of my concern and we prayed that all would turn out right. It ended up getting worse, actually.

After another one of our run-ins, I started to ignore her. I even avoid-ed meal times so I wouldn't have to sit at the table with her. In fact, I went on a week-long fast in an effort to deal with it all. All the while this was happening, whenever I met a new lady I would still be asking the Lord, "Is this the one?"

At the end of my week of praying and fasting, I was walking up the stairs to enter the front door of the house, where Christine was sitting on the steps talking to a friend. I acknowledged her friend but ignored Chris-tine, and walked into the house. I felt a bit rotten doing that, and later went to apologize to her. I guess you the reader have worked all this out a lot quicker than I ever did. One thing led to another and yet another, till even-tually, Chris and I were boyfriend and girlfriend. Sixteen months later, we married.

So, that is how the Lord sent my wife to me. Fortunately the Lord had warned me, because Christine was a member of the household, which meant she was where I was not looking, and I tried pretty hard not to look.

What a blessing for the Lord to send me a wife. I actually married the woman God had chosen for me and it's been a blessing knowing that. I think it's been a blessing for her, too.

So, there I was, laying what I saw as my need (for a wife) before the Lord, and in yet another twinkling of an eye moment, he called me to my knees to guide my looking. I do wonder sometimes what would have happened if I had been too lazy to get out bed to listen to him. I'm guessing, Chris would have thrown herself prostate on the ground, grabbing my ankles and begging me to marry her. (Dear reader . . . .sorry for that last sentence but I want to see Chris's face when she reads it!)

Chapter 14

Opening Windows

Since arriving at Jubilee Fellowship, (Jubes), my Christian life had moved from strength to strength. Oh yes, I had my ups and downs, and failures and successes, but overall, I believed I was heading in the right direction.

In my early days at Jubes, I had just sat in the teaching and services and did not really do much else. Often, I was the first person there, so I used to get the church key from its hiding place, and unlock the door and just sit on a pew, waiting for everyone else to arrive. One day I was sitting there as usual, and the lord said to me, "Open the windows."

It was often hot in the church, and opening the windows would help, so why I had never thought about it, I don't know. Even so, I just sat there. I sort of had an attitude that it was not my job to open the windows, and that someone else could do that. But the lord said it again, "Open the windows." No matter how small the task may seem to us, the lord knows the worth of it.

When I started earnestly seeking God more fully in my life, I asked the lord to show me the work he had for me. By his grace, the lord was now speaking to me of the work he had for me: I was to open windows. Well, it was a bit more than just opening windows, but not much more.

Before I started unlocking the church, people often turned up, only to find it still locked and inaccessible. I was one of those people. Now, I could see it was the Lord's plan for me to arrive early, find the key and open the doors, and in summer, the windows also to let in the fresh air. This I started doing regularly. I told no one, and I didn't ask for permission. I just quietly and as unobtrusively as possible, went about being obedient to God.

Over a period of time, and unbeknown to myself, my actions had been noticed. Having been seen to be responsible, I was asked if I would be a support person to Helen, the Sunday School teacher. I accepted, and supported her for one year. Then, I became responsible for oversight of the Sunday School for a year. After that year, I began to occasionally preach in the church. Whilst continuing with preaching, I became a small group leader and a support person to the eldership (the church had no sole pastor and was run by elders). The next move was to eldership. This may not sound like an astounding rise to the dizzy heights of success, as some may have experienced. But I know one thing for sure, if I had been too proud or disobedient and not been prepared to open windows, I doubt I would have ever proceeded beyond just warming a pew. I had learned that the task God has for us, no matter how insignificant it may seem to us, is often that which prepares us for our next step of the journey.

Jubes then sponsored me on a twelve month, full-time training course with Teen Challenge, which I managed to do by taking twelve months leave without pay from my normal work in the stores at the Transport Department. I did the course, and went back to work with a sense of achievement, and willingness to be God's person in that workplace.

After another year or so, and with a sense of the will of God, and in consultation with the eldership, I left my job and went to Bible College. I needed some extra income, so Chris and I prayed for a part-time, paid position in a ministry situation. Such opportunities were as rare as hen's teeth, yet within days, I received a call from Claude, the Executive Director of Teen Challenge (TC) saying there was a part-time paid position available. The role was as a Youth Worker at the Youth Emergency Shelter, Hebron House, and, as I had already been involved there, I was very excited. I got the job, which involved three, twenty-four-hour shifts every two weeks, and it fitted well with my Bible College timetable. After twelve months or so, I became the new full-time Director of Hebron House. This was amazing, as it was a position I had wanted to apply for a few years before, but the lord had told me I was not to seek the job at that time. I stayed as Director of Hebron, for over two years, which at the time was the longest anyone had held the position. Eventually, the day came when the Lord had spoken to me about resigning, and so I did with no other job to go to. Then, before I left Teen Challenge, the funded position of Social Worker within TC, became available. Amazingly, after putting a request in to the Government, TC was allowed to employ me on the Social Workers grant from the government, with the provision that if I left, it would have to be used for a fully qualified social worker. So, I stayed at TC and became the Training and Development Director, and ran the Telephone Counselor Training Course, and did some counseling and the oversight of Hebron House.

As well as my church life and work life going ahead in leaps and bounds, our marriage was too. Chris had a small inheritance, and we used it as a deposit on a little house in an outer Brisbane suburb, called Inala. The area had a bad reputation, and people advised us not to live there, but it was one of the few suburbs where we could afford to buy. Another benefit was that we did not want to take out a bank loan, as we were not sure what the future would hold, and we managed to get a Housing Commission Loan. The maximum we could borrow was small, but the benefit was that no matter what your wage, you only paid twenty-five percent of it in repayments. We thought this was great, as it meant that even if we were on low income, we would not lose our home, so long as we kept up the small minimum payment.

We had a wonderful five years in Inala. We had a lovely Christian couple living next door on one side, and a gracious retired lady on the other, whose little grandson would just stand and watch me do whatever I did in my yard at any particular time. He never spoke to me, just contentedly stared at me.

Eventually, the day came when we believed the Lord was telling us to sell the house and be available to move for Him. We did not know what this fully meant, but we sold the house and moved nearer to work and church.

At this same time, there were issues within Jubes. The eldership had narrowed itself down to just two, being myself and a guy called Peter. There seemed to be some undertones of unrest within the church. I still don't understand to this day what the issues fully were, but it came to a head at a fellowship meeting to discuss how the church would move forward. It seemed as if people wanted leadership, but not to be led in a specific way. They wanted teaching, but not to be taught things they didn't want to hear. They wanted worship, but not organized worship. To me it just seemed as if they wanted a social club, and not a church. By the time the meeting had come around, I could not stand up and address everyone. I just heard a few comments, and that was all I could take. I just wept and wept. I was not even sure why I was weeping, as there was no single issue that seemed to stand out, except to say my heart felt somewhat broken. I needed time out and Chris and I started attending the local Anglican Church at Bardon, under Reverend Ian McCalister. Ian was a lovely man and very supportive at the time.

Around this same time, Teen Challenge was having issues with staffing a new Rehabilitation Center. Tod and Julianne Berry had arrived from the USA to give their time as workers in the new facility, which was located about an hour's drive north of Brisbane. The only problem was that the center had no Director, so Chris and I wondered if I should apply from within for the position of director of the new center. We decided to go away for a weekend to the Gold Coast, and spend some time in prayer, away from all the usual distractions. We returned with a distinct sense that the lord wanted me to apply for the job. Just to be sure, I told the lord I would apply for the position if Claude raised the matter with me first, otherwise I would not say anything. Each Monday morning, Claude and I would have a meeting (as I was now second in charge at TC), to compare our diaries and plan the week. Claude usually led this time, and as we always had a lot to do, we would normally just get right into discussion and planning. This particular Monday, Claude seemed quiet and even hesitant to speak. Eventually he just blurted out, "What would you think about applying for the Director job at the new center?" It was then that I could tell him my side of the story.

I applied for the job. I went to the board meeting as a member of the board, and having come through the ranks at Teen Challenge. I was in a very strong position to be accepted. I was asked to leave the meeting while the rest of the board discussed my application. I returned to the meeting to be told I had not been successful. I felt shattered. I really just felt so gutted and when I told Chris, she was surprised too. I was asking myself over and over, "Why?" The lord had said apply for the job. Did I not hear the lord? Is my heavenly father just playing a game with me? The thing is, I was doing all this thinking, and trying to work it all out in my head, without taking it to the lord in prayer. As soon as I realized this, I prayed and asked the lord what went wrong. After I said to him, "You said to apply for the job!" Immediately the lord answered with "Yes, I did say to apply for the job, but I never said you'd get it." As soon as I knew that, I felt at peace and knew the will of God for my life was at work, and a few days later I discovered why.

I used to subscribe to a Christian magazine called, "On Being". I have never been much of a reader, but subscribed mainly to help the organization who published it, plus Chris enjoyed reading it. In the midst of all that was happening, the magazine arrived, and I started reading it. I noticed an advertisement to rent a mud-brick house in Lorne, Victoria for very cheap rent, for around three months. As soon as I read it, the lord spoke to my heart and said, "I want you to go and live there." It was not such a foreign idea, as we had friends in Lorne with whom Chris had worked in the old Teen Challenge Rehabilitation Center that had closed down. I was very sure the lord had spoken clearly to me. I told him going there was fine by me but as a confirmation I asked him to let Chris know that we should go and rent the house, but I would say nothing to Chris, unless she said something first. It had to be from the lord. A few days later I was pottering in the front yard, and Chris came and stood in the doorway with the magazine in her hands.

"Have you seen this advertisement for a house to rent in Lorne?" That's where Roy and Lyn live." I just glanced in her direction and acknowledged I had seen it, but made no further comment and carried on pottering. Chris turned and started to walk back into the house and then turned around again and said; "I think the Lord wants us to go there."

I needed no other encouragement. It was clearly the will of God for us. I called the number on the advertisement, and connected to a man named David, and explained our interest. When I told him we had friends in Lorne, he asked who they were. When I said Lyn and Roy, he started laughing, so I figured he most probably knew them. Not only did he know them, but they were actually having dinner right there and then, with him and his wife Angie. It was an exciting moment. Chris and I each had a quick chat with Lyn and Roy, and then I was put back on to David.

Over the next few days, it was decided that we definitely would take up the rental offer for three months in Lorne. It seemed obvious at the time, that I was experiencing a level of burnout, and needed some time to really rest, recover and seek the Lord for the future, and to spend some quality time with my somewhat neglected wife. Three months sounded perfect.

As we reflected on the previous few months since the Lord has asked us to sell our house and be prepared to move we could see the incredible hand of God in all that had happened. Three distinct things had taken place that had made our decision to go to live in Lorne possible.

Firstly, we had left our church, which we never thought we would want to leave. It was gut wrenching, to say the least, but had to be done. Secondly, we were prepared to leave Brisbane to take the Teen Challenge job in the new rehab. I loved Brisbane and never really thought about leaving, until I thought about going to the rehab, and especially so, when God said to apply for the job, our hearts had been prepared to leave. Considering leaving Brisbane also meant being prepared to leave the Teen Challenge I had known. Not getting the new position did really hurt at the time, but on reflection, it was all part of letting go of familiar things, and the preparation of our hearts. I thought I would have been at TC for many more years, but because our hearts and minds had been prepared, saying yes to Lorne and leaving everything else behind, no longer mattered. It just seemed so right in the Lord to go.

The will of God seemed so strong, at that time that I remember setting off for Lorne in our old beat up HJ Holden, feeling as if I could drive through brick walls. Nothing could stop us getting there, because I knew it was one-hundred percent what God wanted. Yet again, a number of twinkling of an eye moments, guiding mine and now Chris's life. The one overriding fact for me in the whole journey, was saying yes to God to open windows. It seemed to me, the rest of the journey unfolded, by accepting the initial work God gave me to do. When God gives it, no task is too small or insignificant in the kingdom of God. We may never know what one small step of obedience to God may lead to, unless we take the first step.

Chapter 15

Far Away from the Crowd

The trip to Lorne included what ended up being two job interviews, well sort of. On the way there, we were going to spend some much-needed time for Chris with her mom and dad in Newcastle. We ended up staying with them for around six weeks. I had read of a ministry called Close To the Edge Ministries (CTEM), and they were advertising for someone to work with troubled youth. I'd made contact with them, and was told they would be partnering with a Uniting Church in Sydney, who would also be providing the accommodation for the successful applicant. We arranged for me to catch up with the leader of CTEM, and the Minister of the Uniting Church, for a couple of days, and I was to provide a lecture on drug use at a training weekend they were having. We also, more out of interest than anything else, visited Teen Challenge in New South Wales on their rural rehabilitation center to see how they ran their program.

The time in Sydney went well, and I was told the job with CTEM was mine if I wanted it. I said I would let them know in due course, after a time of prayer and seeking the lord. But I had already negotiated that I would not be available until I had my three months break in Lorne. It was really good to visit Teen Challenge NSW, and I was greatly encouraged to meet the staff and see the work they were doing.

The drive to Lorne was an experience, to say the least. After living in Brisbane for fourteen years, I had forgotten how cold it could still get in Australia. We drove to Lorne via an inland route, and had a contact in Glenn Innes, where we could stay overnight. The contact was provided by CTEM, and was the minister at the local Uniting Church, (whose wife happened to be the sister of one of my wife's former boyfriends). We turned up at the front door of the Manse, and were asked to park on the open field behind the house. We drove around the back of the house and could only park about the length of a football field from the back door. We jumped out of the car, and had the shock of our life. It was *freezing!* We were dressed in near-tropical gear as we had no winter clothes to speak of that were any use for real winter weather. The cold was so sharp it literally took our breath away. We had stepped out into an icy cold wind, which we discovered later the locals describe as, "blowing off the mountains." We were so taken aback, we ran for the house in shock and laughter. Our poor yellow Labrador, Jess, did not know what hit her. There she was in her fur coat and sitting there shivering. We survived the experience, and woke up to a light covering of snow all around.

The beginning of the next stage of our journey was difficult too, as we had no heater in the car. We put towels around our hands to drive, and kept calling into service stations to see if they had any gloves for sale, but given it was nearly the end of winter, everywhere was sold out. Fortunately, once we hit the lowlands again, it wasn't so bad.

Arriving in Lorne, we drove along the main street and turned right onto Bay Street to receive the shock of our life. We could not believe how steep it was. Our HJ was pulling a small trailer, and we felt as if the car could flip over backwards onto the trailer. I don't remember ever driving up Bay Street again. Even when we were established in Lorne, if we walked up Bay Street we would get halfway up, we would have to walk backwards to reach the top. It was steep!

Arriving at Springwood was lovely. It was a hidden away acreage, with a long driveway access. From the street, you would not know it was there. Founded by Wilf and Elvie, Springwood had three mud-brick houses on the property. They had two sons, David and Peter. Wilf and Elvie lived in the largest house, which was two stories, and the first one visitors would see when driving into the property. They provided accommodation on both levels. Peter, and his wife Alison, were in the small single-story house, which looked quite idyllic in its flowery, garden setting. David, and his wife Angie, had the house we were going to live in, which was a two story house, but the lower level was mainly a garage and storage, and a small flat. Wilf and Elvie had founded Springwood as a retreat for those who needed respite from the business of life. The buildings had been built over time, by the family and many volunteers. The ministry had blessed many people over the years, and had many faithful supporters and friends.

Everyone seemed lovely, and with Lyn and Roy and their children close by, there was a real sense of community, love, and friendship. The rent was minimal for us, but I still needed to do some work to earn income, so I helped Roy a little in his painting business, and picked up some bits and pieces of gardening work. Three months seemed to pass very quickly as Chris and I were really appreciating two or three hour walks through beautiful rainforest, taking in the fauna, waterfalls, and wildlife. The whole experience of bush walking in that area touched us so much, that it felt as if creation itself was directly ministering to us, and bringing refreshment to our spirit and soul. Mentally and emotionally it seemed a long way from the stress of Teen Challenge, church leadership, and being busy sometimes up to seven nights a week.

As the end of the three months drew near, Dave and Angie approached us with an offer to rent the house for a further 12 months. This had not been in our plans, and the weekly rental for the three-month period had been very reasonable, but now it would be rising significantly. It was understandable they could get more rent for the place, but we needed to pray about our future as we were not inclined to think we would be staying in Lorne for a further twelve months. Having prayed, we received a direction we were not expecting. The sense we had in the lord was that we should say no to Dave and Angie's offer, but still remain longer in Lorne. We gave our answer to Dave and Angie, and now we had to find somewhere to live.

The next day, as Chris was working part time at the local supermarket, she said she would call into the real estate office on the way home, to see what our options were. While Chris was at work, I spent some time in prayer, and I got a specific answer from the lord. When Chris returned home, she looked somewhat downcast. It seemed there were not many houses available for rent, and those that were available had rents we could not afford. I told her the answer the Lord had given me in prayer, which was very simple and direct. We were not to go looking for somewhere to rent, because the opportunity would come to us, without our going out to find it. Plus, we were not to tell anyone we were looking for somewhere to live, unless they asked us. We both agreed with it, and waited to see what the Lord was going to do. It was easy to wait at first, because we had a few weeks before we had to move out of Dave and Angie's place. But as the weeks dwindled away, it was harder and harder not to tell others we needed somewhere to live. But, we just kept trusting in the word of the lord to us.

Now and again, Springwood would have a community BBQ, which locals and visitors were invited to attend. At one such BBQ, I was standing there talking to Harry, who I had met a few times before, and who lived in a big wooden house along the driveway into Springwood. He was involved with the Springwood Community, but his dwelling was on an adjoining property. He asked me how long we were staying at Dave and Angie's place, and I explained we would be moving out soon, but I did not say when. Looking back, strangely enough, no one else to that point in time had asked me that question. He asked me where we were going to live, and I was really tempted to say we have not looked for anywhere, but I had to answer carefully to honor the lord's word to me, so I just said I was not sure yet. He then told me he had a cousin who had a holiday house down on George Street, who only used it mainly for family holidays at Christmas and New Year breaks. This seemed like the answer to the word from the lord that the opportunity would come to us without our going out to find it (was this the twinkling of an eye moment?). Harry explained his cousin was in Lorne at the moment, and he arranged for us to go and see him and check the house out.

Arriving at Harry's cousins house, we knocked on the front door but there was no answer, so we walked around the back and up onto a deck. George Street is one big hill, and this house was about half way up the hill, and once on the deck we had incredible views along the Great Ocean Road heading towards Geelong, and a near hundred and eighty degree ocean view. Chris and I just looked at each other and without saying a word, communicated that it would be wonderful but out of our price league. Just then Harry's cousin and family entered the property from the corner of the back yard, and immediately saw us on the deck.

Harry's cousin, Jeff, and wife Pauline, were lovely people with three gorgeous children. They had just walked up from the beach and were laughing and joking with each other and they seemed such a positive family. We all chatted politely on the deck for a while and then Jeff got down to business. He suggested what the rent could be, but lowered it a little, given that they may stay in the granny flat section of the house sometimes. It was still about three times as much as I was earning a week, and way out of our reach. Jeff asked what I was doing for work and I shared about my painting work with Roy, and gardening work and some handyman work I was now starting to pick up. Jeff was really interested, and asked if I might be able to paint the house and granny flat inside and out, do some repairs around the place, build a fence, and put in stepped garden beds with a sprinkler system. This sounded ideal to me.

We worked out a deal that every ten hours work would be one week's rent. Chris and I could hardly believe this incredible provision provided by the lord, and all without going out to find it ourselves. We ended up staying there from February to November, and I worked off all the rent, and when we left, Jeff and Pauline were so happy, they paid our final gas and electricity bills. It was such a blessing for us to live there. Anyone who visited us was amazed, because when they arrived at the house, they could not see the sea, but as soon as they entered the house, they could see down the hallway and the sea view immediately struck them. There were often sighs of amazement.

The really wonderful thing about it all was that we did not have to go and find somewhere to live, because the lord sent it to us. We just had to wait on his timing, and it was provided for us in the twinkling of an eye.

Soon after we moved in to Jeff and Pauline's place, I got my second job offer, which was totally unexpected. It was from Teen Challenge NSW. It seems my visit there was a success, and they were offering me a position at the Rehabilitation Center. It was a bit confusing though. The Director of TC did not say he was offering me a job, but he said he was offering me a calling. Ok, so I was being offered a paid position that was not a job, but was a calling. I never liked talk that was not clear and left things a bit ambiguous and somewhat confusing, so needless to say, I did not like the way the offer was put. I had seen quite a few Christians "burned" over the years with promises of jobs or housing or both, only to see them disappointed when they pack up and leave for fresh pastures, and then find the pastures are not as anticipated, or nothing like what was described. I wasn't particularly worried about that but for me when terms like "calling" and "job" are somewhat confusing and it puts up a red flag. I told him I would pray about it and be in touch in due course. After prayer, I had a very clear idea in my mind of what I wanted to ask, and the things I needed to be clear of before I could give TC my answer. I made a list of questions that I believed I would need the answers to for me to make a properly informed decision. Chris did not particularly like my list, and thought I might discourage them from hiring me by asking so many questions. Given that I had no real future work prospects, and I had already turned down the offer from CTTE, I could understand her concern. I explained to her that even if the answers were not the ones I wanted to hear, they would be important to know and a part of our decision-making process, before deciding to take the position or not. This was after prayer, and I believe it was the way forward in the lord.

I gave the Director the list of questions that I would need answers for. These included such practical things as: Where would we be living in relation to the residents? What would my working hours be each day? How many days a week would I be working? How many days a week could I have away from the property? Along with the general questions regarding wages, holidays, sick leave, etc. I think my concern at the time was that the term, "calling" could be abused. If it was a "job", then it's got terms and conditions. But a calling is different, that can mean you have to work at any time needed, after all, it's not a job but a call from God on your life, and how can you ever say "No" to God. I just did not want to end up in a situation leading to burn-out, with the view that it's what I signed up for, so it was my own fault.

The Director and I chatted on the phone, and though he sounded a little put out by my list, he said he would get back to me. He never did. The next thing I knew was when their newsletter arrived in the mail and I discovered he had given the position to someone else. It was fine by me, and I was at peace with the whole thing, because I was not sure I was ready to work for Teen Challenge again just yet, or if indeed, I ever would be.

Whilst Lorne was a time of long walks, wonderful times with Chris and friends, and learning just what mischief a yellow Labrador would get up to if food was involved, it was also a time of seeking the Lord and wanting to know his will for our life.

The year was drawing to an end, and Jeff and Pauline would need the house back in late November. We had no idea what we were going to do, but given that we felt so much in the will of God, we just plodded along expecting he would guide us. And guidance did come.

Rather surprisingly, we were approached by Springwood with an offer. Our time living on the Springwood property had been very positive, and we had joined in many of the activities associated with the community. They even celebrated their twenty-fifth anniversary while we were there, and something very special happened out of the blue. The Lord gave me a song for their anniversary celebration party. I was not, and still am not a musician. But I enjoy a plonk on the guitar, and the song came to me without trying. I just believe it was of the Lord. Here are the words to it;

The Springwood Song

Rest my weary mind
Lay down my cares
Feel the cool night air
Unpack my wares
Meet the local folks
See the ocean view
Hear the parrots chirping
Everything seems new

Chorus
In Springwood
Far away from the crowd
In Springwood
Away from all that is loud
There's a peace that I can feel
A tranquility so real
And I thank you Lord
For bringing me to Springwood

Wilf and Elvie
Pete and Al'
Dave and Ange
Others as well
There's smiling faces here
Each person is so dear
And in each smiling face
I see Your wondrous grace

Repeat Chorus

Seeking you Lord
That's why I'm here
To seek Your face
And to draw near
To call upon Your name
That is my only aim

Among the tall gum trees
I know You're here with me

Repeat Chorus

I can honestly say I am still thankful.

The offer from Springwood was for us to move on to the property for up to twelve months, and assist them in putting together a document of what Springwood was all about. Together with this, we would help them develop a way forward for the community. After prayer and discussion, it was an offer we accepted. Wilf and Elvie moved to the downstairs of their house, and Chris and I moved in upstairs. We had regular meetings, and discussions varied from personal and family issues, to life in the broader community of local churches, and Lorne itself.

It was a very challenging year, and one I am happy to say the lord had gifted and equipped me for. Many issues were resolved, and a document was put together with a vision for the future. Rather than being a community on the hill and just attending their own worship meetings, it was decided that the community would relate more closely with the local Uniting and Anglican Churches. The outcome was that one Sunday each month was devoted to attending the Uniting Church, and another Sunday for the Anglican Church. Two Sundays of the month were for worship at Springwood, which visitors had come to expect. This worked really well, and took away some suspicions about Springwood from many locals. There were benefits for all parties.

Once again, we only had a short term "contract" in the Lord, and we had no idea where we would be going once the twelve months were up, so Chris and I had started spending time in prayer for our future. Before long, we did find direction, thanks to a visit to Youth With A Mission (YWAM), in South Australia, and due to Springwood's involvement in the local churches.

Chris' best friend, Helen, and her husband Mark, were the leaders of the YWAM base in Adelaide. Chris and Helen had grown up as next-door neighbors, and would talk to each other through their bedroom windows. They became Christians within about three months of each other, when they were sixteen.

Helen and Mark had invited us to the YWAM base to stay in their guest room, and have a holiday. We were going to drive there, so it would be another little adventure on the road for us. A few days before we left, I went off to do one of my gardening jobs, and as I was weeding away the lord spoke to me. I was excited to get back to Chris and tell her what the Lord had said. As I walked into the house, Chris was just getting off the telephone from Helen, with a disappointed look on her face. On enquiring, she explained how Helen had just told her we could not have the special guest room on our visit, as a leader from YWAM was visiting and would have priority for the room. I then told Chris not to worry, as the Lord had just told me that on our visit to Adelaide we would meet someone who would have a word for us about our future. Now, I was wondering if this YWAM leader could be the person.

On arrival at the YWAM base, we briefly met Helen and Mark, and went to their rooms to chat with them and the YWAM leader. Helen and Mark had business to attend to and apologized as they left the three of us for a short while. The three of us chatted away for a few minutes, sharing where we were at in life, and suddenly the YWAM leader said, "I don't know what the Lord has in mind for you, but it's more than where you are at the moment." That was it, the word for us from the Lord. I knew immediately in my heart that was meant for us. Mark and Helen returned, the leader left, and I don't recall ever seeing him again. It had be a twinkling of an eye moment.

So, now we had a sense that there was change ahead for us, and we were assuming it did not include Springwood, or staying in Lorne. The next part of the direction came from our involvement with the local Uniting Church.

I used to preach at Jubilee Fellowship in Brisbane, and while in Lorne, I was invited to preach a number of times at St. Cuthbert's Uniting Church. Then, one day totally out of the blue, the Minister, Duncan, challenged me to become a Minister of the Word. This would mean attending Bible College, and gaining a degree in Theology, and then applying to be ordained as a Minister of the Word in the Uniting Church. This would be with the intention of going into full-time ministry in the Church. I had thought a number of times in the past about gaining a degree in Theology, but the lord never opened up the way for me to do it. Maybe this was now the right timing. After prayer I agreed to look into it, and take a tentative step. I was a bit wary, as I had never really been committed to a particular denomination in the past. Yes, I had attended a mainline church here and there, but I had never become a member of any. The Parish Council validated Duncan's endorsement of me, and I arranged to meet with someone in Melbourne to discuss the possibility.

When I arrived at my interview, the person I needed to talk to was on the telephone having a good laugh with someone. We could see each other from where I was sitting, and upon finishing his call, he motioned me to enter the room. His demeanor changed immediately. In the twinkling of an eye he went from laughing and joking to looking me up and down with a stern look on his face, as if asking himself, "What have we got here?" I don't know why he looked like that, and of course I can't be sure that is what he was thinking, but it was an abrupt change and it was as if the mood in the room changed, too.

We didn't talk for long. I would guess, thinking back, that it was only five to ten minutes. I basically told him why I was there and he answered that he thought I should not apply to become a Minister of the Word, but to become a Lay Pastor instead. That was it really. I was out of the room nearly as quickly as I went in. I was a bit dazed, to say the least. I'd travelled for a couple of hours to get to Melbourne, took half an hour or so to find the appointment room, and now after a few short minutes, I was on my way. I wasn't particularly fazed by what he said, but just felt a bit put out by the process. This had all been committed to the Lord in prayer, so my main thing now was to seek what the Lord was saying through all this.

Duncan encouraged me, that given my experience maybe being a Lay Pastor would be good, and could still be a stepping stone to ordination. It's at this point that the hand of the Lord seemed to really take hold of the situation, and give guidance that was fundamentally out of my control.

One day soon after, I was looking through the "On Being" magazine, and there was a position being advertised for a Lay Pastor at Jindabyne in the Snowy Mountains district of New South Wales. It said Lay Preachers could apply. So, I figured I was a lay person, and I preached so there was nothing to stop me applying, so I did. I sent off a brief resume of my Christian experience, and low and behold, they were interested in talking further with me. I talked on the phone with them a few times, and all seemed very positive and moving in the right direction. That was until they asked me the fateful question, "When did you get your lay preachers certificate?" I had not realized that to be called a "Lay Preacher" in the Uniting Church was a little more involved than just not being ordained and preaching. It was an actual course, run over four semesters with an official church qualification at the end of it. They asked me to start the course as soon as possible, and they would talk to the church hierarchy in Sydney to see if that would be enough to get things rolling. So, I did my bit and started the course with a couple of other people, under Duncan's oversight and direction. Then I got the news that I would need the full qualification to be able to apply to be a Lay Pastor.

I went to the next Lay Preachers study meeting somewhat dismayed, both by my own lack of being organized in the first place, although I was well known by others to be over the top organized, and because what I wanted now, seemed impossible. The news that I would not be able to apply to be a Lay Pastor for possibly two more years, was a bit of a downer to say the least. It had all been moving along so well that the outcome, to me at least, seemed to be somewhat inevitable. Now, I was having a moment of despair. I went to the meeting, and as we all sat around the table, Duncan, with whom I had not discussed the latest development yet, asked each of us how things were going with the course. When it came to my turn, I said it was fine, but I was somewhat disappointed as I had discovered I could not complete the course as quickly as I had thought. Duncan's immediate feedback was that there was provision for a person to take the complete course, all four subjects, in one semester if it was deemed appropriate. I asked who the person was who could make that decision, and he informed me it was up to the local minister, who just happened to be him. As a Minister of the Word, and my immediate Pastor, he could make the decision based on his personal judgment. To cut a long story short, I completed the whole course in six weeks and gained my certificate. I was excited to call Jindabyne and tell them the good news. However, the news from their end was not so good.

Given that they wanted to employ a Lay Pastor, they could not "call" one themselves. They could "call" a Minster of the Word and interview, and potentially offer them a position, but for Lay Pastors, it was different. Lay Pastors came under the authority of the Board of Mission, and were appointed by the board. A Lay Pastor could not pick and choose where they wanted to go, but had to go where they were sent. I discovered they were generally sent to the places that Ministers of the Word would not go, due to extensive travel, or very small townships. As Jindabyne were interested in appointing me, the Board of Mission informed them that if I wanted to apply to be a Lay Pastor, I would be interviewed in Sydney, and if given a position, Jindabyne would be considered as a placement. With this understanding, I applied, and arranged to drive to Sydney for the interview, with a stop-over in Jindabyne to meet the parish members and preach.

Visiting Jindabyne was lovely. The town and district are beautiful, and the church members were warm, loving, and accepting. One of the things I found funny there was that when I preached and looked over the heads of the congregation, I could see the lake through the back wall, which was mainly full of windows. It was a great view, but a little distracting, as there were boats, and people water skiing, going back and forth on the water. I mentioned this to a parishioner, who also preached or led services sometimes, and he said it would be really distracting when someone from church was on the lake instead of attending the service, and would be skiing and waving to the church whilst going from side to side across the lake. We left there very positive that we would see them all again soon. We never did get back.

The interview went really well in Sydney, and I was offered a position, but because of my Teen Challenge background, and involvement in drug and alcohol counseling, they wanted me to go somewhere else: Wakool. Yes, Wakool, and I guess you, the reader, have never heard of it, just like I hadn't.

But, here was the amazing thing about all this that proved to me God's hand in the whole scenario. I had applied for a job without the qualification, to allow me to apply in the first place. But the job I should not have applied for was also a position that should not have been advertised in the way it was. In some ways, on reflection, the whole thing seemed like a comedy of errors, but the outcome was so of God, that it could not have all happened without him pulling it all together. The whole process of beginning to pray about our future, and the way the direction came, was full of twinkling of the eye moments. We returned to Springwood and finished off our time there, whilst preparing for the new adventure ahead.

Chapter 16

Pastor

Arriving in Wakool seemed so much in the will of God for us. Being a full-time pastor was a dream come true, as people had often said I would be a pastor one day, but I could never see it happening. Now, by God's grace, it was.

When I first arrived, at least one parishioner laughed at me, because I said it was great that I was going to get paid to preach. I just thought it was amazing to think I was going to be paid to do what I loved. It's such a privilege to share the Word of God with others, and encourage them to walk closely with the lord. From the first time I was asked to prepare and preach a sermon, I knew immediately I had been gifted by the Lord to serve him in that way. Though Christian life calls us to serve others, I have never felt more like I am serving the lord than when I preach. It's simply a gift from God, and even though it can be taxing to stand in front of people who may not necessarily want to hear all I have to say, I enjoy exercising it. Of course, there is more to being a pastor than just preaching.

Being a part of a mainline church was a real challenge for me. I had never been used to such things as singing hymns, or representing the church in the community, Presbytery meetings, funerals, weddings, etc. Even being reverently respected by some members of the church and local community, simply because I was a pastor, was foreign to me and not anything I wanted. But the truth was that some people treated me differently, because I was the pastor. The one lesson I learned is that Christians come in all shapes and sizes, with many varied doctrinal beliefs and lifestyles. A bunch of sheep who need a shepherd. As we all do.

The foibles and challenges of leading a congregation, was indeed a trial at times, and I had four of them. I had congregations at Wakool, Moolamein, Caldwell and Burraboi. We lived in Wakool, and the town had a church building and a congregation of around fifteen to twenty regular attendees. Caldwell was about a twenty-five kilometer (15 miles) drive from Wakool. There was no town there, and no church building, other than a tin shed. It was used as a community meeting place that people from the farms would use for events. It had a small congregation of five to ten regular attendees. I once preached there to just two people, and I can tell you that was a real challenge, especially when one of the two was Chris, who had heard the sermon already! The place, itself, could hold up to around one-hundred people, and often did for a Christmas service or some community events.

Moulamein was about a sixty-five kilometer (40 miles) drive from Wakool, which made for a real dash in the car some Sunday mornings, and especially so when it was the Sunday for the one hundred kilometer (62 miles) trip from Caldwell to Moulamein. It had a traditional wooden church building, and generally, the congregation was around fifteen regulars.

Burraboi was about eighteen kilometers (11 miles) from Wakool, and had a lovely wooden church, and around ten to fifteen regular attendees. Burraboi had a rice mill and a primary school, and half-dozen or so houses.

Throughout the week, much of my time was spent on the road and, depending on events and their locations, I could sometimes do over five-hundred kilometers. This was not difficult, as a round trip to Moulamein from Wakool was one-hundred and thirty kilometers. By attending church on Sunday, Parish Council on Tuesday, and Primary School Scripture on Wednesday, I had already done around three-hundred and ninety kilometers in just three drives, in only three of my six working days. It did not take much time for the kilometers to add up. Travel times can be a significant factor for country pastors. Sometimes leaving at sunrise, it would be a five hour drive on some narrow country roads to get to a Presbytery Meeting, and then the same drive home at night. Then it was up and out again the next day for three services.

Really, the distance between the congregations was all part of what needed to happen, when small churches were required to band their financial resources together to employ a Pastor. I'm sure if each center could afford to employ their own individual pastor, I think they would have. So, my life as a country Pastor was very much a life on the road, going to the congregations, farms, and community activities.

We ran Kid's Clubs at Wakool, Moulamein, and Caldwell, and they were very successful. They were extremely tiring, as they went for three hours at a time. Many was the time Chris and I would arrive home to just stare blankly at the lounge room wall as we re-cooperated. As there was not much for primary school-age children in the small communities, as well as being a form of outreach, Kid's Club was also a real service to the families. We had School Scripture in Moulamein, Wakool, and Burraboi Primary Schools and had some great times with some very creative scripture lessons.

The really good thing though, was the people. After all, the people are the church, not the buildings that the people meet in. I saw lives growing in the Lord, young people dedicating themselves to God, and even experienced a significant healing from cancer.

One member of our Burraboi congregation had a history with cancer, and had been doing well for years, until out of the blue there was a negative diagnosis. The cancer had returned, and he urgently needed to go to Sydney for surgery. We arranged a time of prayer for healing before he left. Some of us, about six as I recall, met together to lay hands on the man and pray for him. I took the approach of initially committing the overall time to God, and led everyone in communion. I spoke about the need to silently confess our sin and take it to the cross and come afresh before God, forgiven and cleansed. As unconfessed sin can be a barrier to drawing close to God in prayer, I felt this was necessary. We laid hands on the man, and in obedience to the Word of God, I anointed him with oil for healing, and then we prayed over him. Now let me be clear here. This man attended church regularly, but was not the sort of person to show any outward excitement, or to wave his hands around in worship. I suppose I could say he was generally a quiet, undemonstrative man. It took us all by surprise that as we said, "Amen," he suddenly shouted out, "I am healed", and punched the air in excitement. We were somewhat taken aback. A few days later, his wife called to tell me the news from Sydney. Her husband had been admitted, and a further test was undertaken to confirm where and how large the cancer was. Apparently, he had been prepared for the operation with lines drawn on his body for where the incisions would be made. The specialist came back and said there was no need for the operation. They could no longer find signs of cancer. He had been right. He was healed!

Our three year placement seemed to fly by and we were offered the chance to move to another parish. After prayer, Chris and I sensed another year, at the most, would be good. We were granted another year.

Towards the end of our final year, I was thinking about where we might be moved to by the Board of Mission, and we were open to anywhere, really. As I was thinking on these lines, I happened to pick up a recent copy of the "On Being" magazine. I flicked through its pages, and kept noticing positions vacant for church Pastors. I got a pen, and starting at the front of the magazine, I turned each page looking at the job advertisements, and circling some, while saying things to myself like, "I could do that one." "This one." "That's a possibility." After I had gone all the way through, I put the magazine in the rack and never thought further about it. A few weeks later, I was walking through the lounge room, and a twinkling of an eye moment was sprung upon me. As I walked past the magazine stand, the lord said to me (inner voice of the heart), "Pick up the 'On Being' magazine, and look at the jobs you circled." I picked it up, and began turning the pages. I looked at the first advertisement I had circled and wondered why I would have ever circled that one. I repeated this with the next three or four advertisements, further wondering what I must have been thinking to assume these were jobs I would be suitable for. Then I turned the page and saw the next item, and before I could read it the Lord said to me, "Apply for this one." So I did.

The advertisement was short on details, and did not even mention the name or denomination of the church. All I really knew was the location was Palm Beach in Sydney. This meant absolutely nothing to me, but Chris was pretty excited at the prospect of living there.

Within a couple of weeks, I was on my way to Sydney for an interview for the position of Associate Pastor at St. Mark's, Avalon and St David's, Palm Beach, with the Anglican Church. I had to drive three hours to Wagga Wagga to get my Friday afternoon flight so I could have my interview on the Friday evening, and then fly back to Wagga Wagga the next morning, with the return three hour drive to Wakool. Only our friend, Jenny, at Burraboi knew about the trip, as I did not want to unsettle the parish unnecessarily.

The morning after my interview, I was offered the position. I said I would pray about it and discuss it with my wife and let them know. I accepted the position a few days later.

I'm not sure the Board of Mission was happy with my decision, (I never did get given my reference), and I could understand that, but I could not help it either. God had given me direction, and I had to follow it. It was wonderful to reflect that once again in my life, I was moving to a job that had come from direct guidance from the Lord. We excitedly packed and moved to Sydney.

"I have never moved anyone from one place to another that were so contrasting," said the mover as I opened the door. He was probably right, too. Wakool was a semi desert area, that was flat, and grew rice, thanks to water irrigation. We were now looking down from our flat along Palm Beach, with beautiful sands, and lush green vegetation, with picturesque views of Barrenjoey Lighthouse in the distance. The contrast was so grand for Chris and I, that for the first week we found it difficult to drive around the shoreline, as the hills made us feel somewhat disoriented. The green looked so, green!

The congregation at St David's at Palm Beach was mainly made up or retirees, and had one Sunday morning service a week, usually a Prayer Book service that followed predetermined outlines. St Mark's at Avalon, had an 8:00 am Prayer Book service, a 10:00 am Family Service, and a 6:30 pm Youth and Young Adults Service. At various times, I would be involved in all services, but my main area of responsibility was the evening service. There were challenges for me presenting a prayer book service, as I had never done one before, and it was quite different to my informal style of service preparation and leading. However, I did see the benefits of having a planned format that kept people on track, for keeping to the essential elements for a worship service.

Though we were missing the Wakool Parish people, we were excited at the prospects that lay ahead. We were well received by church members and there was certain freedom in the evening worship style, which was more in keeping with what I was accustomed to. I immediately felt at home in the church. It was an exciting time, and going very well, even though I was asked to take on some tasks, such as primary-school scripture, which, it had been agreed before I started, I would not be doing. I was keen on High School Scripture, and coordinated and gave lessons, but I wanted to leave primary scripture behind. It was not to be so. This was no big deal, except for the time involved in preparation and attendance. I liked to be fully prepared for tasks I took on, and the more that was put in to my week, the less I could prepare properly. I was also asked to do some Anglican Church studies, which put pressure on me, and took a considerable amount of time. There were exams to do and there was one week when I had an exam, in addition to two funerals! I asked the powers that be if I could postpone my exam, but they said there was no provision to do it any other week. I scraped through.

I ran a home group for members of the evening service, and did various counseling and from time to time, community duties. I became very busy in the parish, and was loving my work and the people, but some circumstances began to raise the pain I carried around on the inside. The pain would never fully go away, and would raise its ugly head when I least expected it. After three years in the parish, I was asked to stay another year. I asked the lord for three conditions I wanted changed, otherwise I would not stay longer. Without anyone knowing what I had asked the lord, the three conditions were changed to what I desired. I saw this as a confirmation of God's will for me to stay. Though I expected more discussion on the subject, I somehow agreed to stay another year.

Within about two months of that year, all the three conditions were removed, and I went into a deep depression. I just wanted to die. I can't properly explain how I felt. It was not a selfish attitude in me. It seemed the least change in my circumstances now raised my inner pain level to something I had difficulty coping with. I think the best I can say is, I simply felt the end of the road had come. I was just too tired to think about it, and continue walking in my pain. Each day was a torture for me, on the inside. Not that anyone knew that. I do not understand why the lord allowed it, other than to allow me to make a free will decision on my future. I'm not sure. I hung in there for as long as I could, but it was a very dark period for me. It was like the straw that broke the camel's back, and led to the end of my time there. I resigned. I was in too much inner pain to stay and it would not go away. It was not the fault of any individual or of the parish. The parish was wonderful, and tried to persuade me to stay, but I knew I needed to leave. I had experienced a wonderful three—going on four, years there and no one was to blame for my leaving.

I personally felt a complete failure before God and people. In hindsight, I could have told the parish how I was feeling, and I'm sure they would have been compassionate and helpful, as that's the sort of parish it was. But I left.

As far as my personal inner journey was concerned, I was recognizing more and more clearly the deep sources of my inner pain; two childhood experiences and they're resulting, but as yet not fully recognized consequences. These had sown the seeds of despair into my life. The time was nearing for God to do a fresh, deep and lasting work in my heart.

Chapter 17

My Biggest Personal Battle

Depression. Not understood by many, and suffered by too many. If you have read my previous chapters, you will have seen how God brought transformation in many areas of my life, in the twinkling of an eye. Travelling with depression was a long journey that I knew I had to endure and entrust to my heavenly father. He had told me as much in prayer. When I prayed for my depression to go away, the only answer I sensed in God was that my depression was a "thorn in the flesh." Paul the Apostle wrote to the Corinthians, "Therefore, in order to keep me from becoming conceited, I was given a thorn in my flesh, a messenger of Satan, to torment me." (II Cor. 12:7 NIV)

Now, I am not attempting to put myself on par with the apostle Paul, or to claim that I understand all that Paul means in the above passage of scripture. However, it was clear to me it was something I would need to trust to God's care on a continual, day-by-day basis.

I'm sure not many people understand much at all about this often hidden illness. Let me give some insight into what depression was like for me. Generally "normal" people, (in this case "normal" means those without severe depression), get feeling down about something in their lives, and might say they feel depressed. Then, the next minute, their situation changes and they are able to get on with life. That is, perhaps, a form of depression, but I have found that people in that category rarely seem to understand real depression. They think people with depression can just change their immediate circumstances, maybe get a bit more money, get a new partner, etc., and all the depression ceases. Not so. I'll tell you how debilitating depression was for me, and what it felt like to experience.

Firstly, it was painful. The physical pain I felt was real. It was as if I had a lead weight in the middle of my chest, trying to drag me down. And it would. I remember one morning the pain was so intense as I lay in bed, that as I tried to get out of bed to go to the bathroom, I could only roll out onto the floor, and crawl to the doorway. The weight of pain in my chest was just so debilitating, in a way I cannot describe, that it dragged me to the ground. It was a real pain. The best I can say is that it was an emotional pain, felt physically. It was a pain that took all my energy to fight against and would, at times, leave me exhausted from the struggle. I've found no one understands that type pain, unless they have experienced it. If you have never experienced such pain, then I am genuinely happy for you, but please remember these next two sentences. If someone you know tells you they are depressed and has an inner pain they cannot do anything about, then please, please, listen to them. Get them some help because the pain can lead to something terrible.

This comes to my second point. The pain was so severe that, at times, I just wanted it to stop. How do you stop a pain so deep in your physical person and soul, that it debilitates your day-to-day existence, so that you just long for it to go away at any cost? How do you stop a pain like that? At various times when the depression was most severe, the only option I could see to end the pain was to consider ending my life by suicide. You just want the pain to stop! It's an illogical thought really, but you just think and say to yourself, "at least that way the pain would stop." As illogical as it really was, it started to become so obvious to me that the only way to stop the pain was to stop living. That's what deep-seated psychological and emotional pain does to a person; well it did to me.

Thirdly, I never knew what would start a trip into a depressed state of pain and a sense of despair. I didn't know the triggers that would start it off. I could be sitting around a dinner table with friends, having a wonderful time, when all at once, seemingly out of nowhere, my pain would rise up, and I would begin to feel inexplicable inner anguish. When that occurred, I would immediately retreat deep into my shell. I could only guess that it was something said, or someone's actions that triggered an emotional memory of some sort. I just did not know. I only knew I could be fine one minute, and severely depressed the next. I never knew when it would raise its ugly head. It just would spring up and attack me.

Now the strange thing is this, I was, at this time, a full-time pastor working in the church. I went through a period of about three years, during which the depression was so bad, that I would wake up with pain and pray to my heavenly Father, "Father if you don't protect me today, I will kill myself. The pain is so bad I just want it to come to an end. So, give me this day what I need to survive." I would pray a prayer similar to that most days, during that awful period.

I would not go to a doctor or any professional to deal with the issue, as I firmly believed it was my "thorn in the flesh" that I had to journey with. Through this time, I never once took a sick day from work because of it, shirked my responsibilities, or told anyone what I was truly feeling inside, or let anyone in on my day-to-day battle.

It was a perilous and scary journey for me at times. I remember one day, walking along the side of the road at Palm Beach on Sydney's Northern Beaches with my wife, and a bus was coming along and I really had to fight so hard on the inside not to throw myself in front of it. Chris knew nothing of those thoughts, as I kept quiet about them; I felt I had to protect her from my pain. I'm sure she would never have got into a car with me, had she known how often I just felt like driving head-on into an on-coming car; or just go off the road and over a cliff, or into a tree.

There was a quite amazing aspect to this journey which, on reflection, I still shake my head at. As a pastor, I had people coming for counsel for any number of reasons or situations. During the time of my deepest depressions, the Lord would send me people for counseling who were suffering from some sort of depression. There were appointments when what I was saying to others was so important for me to hear. It really was bizarre at times as the support I gave others, God actually ministered to me. I would sit there sometimes as people opened up to tell my why they had come to see me, and I would be silently praying, "Father, I need help more than them. I'm just where they are at but worse! Give me what I need to say to them as I can't help them." My prayers were always answered in those situations.

People would tell me I was the first person they had ever talked to who they felt had really listened, and heard the cry of their heart. They'd tell me they felt understood at last, and somehow it gave them strength to carry on. Of course, if I felt people needed professional help, I would suggest they seek someone more qualified than myself. But, I can tell you that each one of those counseling times were little twinkling of the eye moments, in which I knew God gave me words to say that ministered to the person — and also to myself.

Each day was a challenge, but one that the Lord got me through. However, eventually the day came when it all felt too much to bear, and I felt I should leave my position at the church. I just explained that it was for personal reasons, and did not elaborate any further than that. I did have some issues with my role at the time, but my depression was the overriding factor in leaving.

I felt a failure. I felt I'd let people down. Deep inside though, I just knew it was the decision I had to make. So, I left the church after nearly four years of ministry there.

I started my own business as a children's entertainer, and settled back in to a more general lifestyle. Nevertheless, my depression continued, and the pain would just not go away. I came to the point where I believed the Lord was telling me to seek some professional help. To be honest, for a long time I had expected another twinkling of an eye moment and instant deliverance, but it didn't happen that way.

I approached a psychologist who attended the new church we were going to, figuring he had been put in my path and was the obvious choice. He said he could not do it, and recommended a female psychologist he knew. I was not sure about talking to a woman on this matter, as I had no idea what could come out, and what I may need to talk about. I arranged to see the person, but really hoped there was not any unknown or hidden sexual stuff to discuss that I was not aware of! I'm happy to say there was not. My only desire and priority in seeing any psychologist was that they be a Christian—and this lady was.

I went to my first appointment, and we just sat and chatted informally at first. I was happy to hear that her approach was not to take a long term view, but rather to look to the next six or so weeks, find solutions to what was bothering me, and treat the problem. The lady asked me about my childhood and upbringing, and my life's journey. Towards the end of the hour, she summed up our time together, and what she felt were the issues I needed to look at and deal with. They were quite succinct. She felt I had issues with loss and grief. Quite simply, the things I had had in my life, but had lost. And the sense of loss of the things I should've had in my life and never did. The grief part related to those two aspects of loss. The grief associated with losing what I did have, and grief that comes from not having that which a person needs for a healthy emotional and balanced life. Before I left, I was given some simple homework to help me think about these things before we got back together again next time.

I can now tell you that I walked out of that meeting wondering if the lady knew what she was talking about. I had been through many trials in my personal life, and had changed a lot and I just could not see how what she was saying was applicable to me. I had so much personal insight and understanding of how I worked that I thought the lady was totally on the wrong track. But fair enough, I would go away and do my homework, and think about what she had said. No harm in that, I thought.

No word of a lie, I could not get back there quickly enough the next week! Each day after the meeting, as I pondered on the homework and things we had talked about, a very clear picture was forming. It was basically so simple, but was at the same time, most powerful in helping me come to terms with deep seated issues that brought on my depression.

A really important area for me to come to terms with was where to lay the blame for things in my life I had actually been blaming myself for. I had always blamed myself for being illegitimate, because that is the message that society had given me over and over. My identity was described in what society used as a swear word, or at the very least an abusive and derogatory term. I was a bastard, and generally in the era I was born into, I was a societal outcast. The thing was, for the whole of my life, I had somehow believed it to be wholly my fault. I blamed myself for everything.

As a child, if there was an argument about money, (and we had these often), I would blame myself, because in my mind, if I was not there, then there would be no money problems. So in effect, the fact that I was born was the problem. My uncles did not want to know me nor my mom, and this was obviously because I was an embarrassment to the family; so it was my fault. My dad's parents didn't want to know me, which was normal, because I would bring shame on them; so it was my fault. Neighbors would look at me strangely, or a new friend's parents would ask about my family, and then discourage me from playing with their children. Just a knowing look or a stare, and I could tell what was in these people's thoughts toward me. All of these thoughts of mine were, of course, totally irrational, and a product of things that had happened to me, and due to the society I grew up in. But, now I came to the time to lay the fault and the blame where it actually belonged.

Mom and Dad had sex out of wedlock and produced a child. That was not my fault. It was something they did, not me. I was the result; the fault was theirs. If any blame was to be attributed, I had to attribute it to them.

Dad's parents had not wanted their son to marry a non-Catholic, and so would not approve of a wedding. It was their problem, and not mine that Dad did not marry Mom. Irrespective of what his parents wished, he was a grown man, and should have made his own decisions. That was his fault, and I was not to blame. I was illegitimate. I was not to blame. It was not my fault!

Together, with putting the blame where it needed to be put, there were also the issues that had affected me growing up with my Great Uncle Colin. Poor guy could not help it. The First World War had left him mentally disabled. He would explode in fits of temper and rage, and such foul and abusive language. I remember a childhood, so often filled with fear and tears. How did I cope with this? I used to go and sit in a corner and draw, and color pictures. I would try to physically and emotionally detach myself from the situation. I would basically withdraw myself, and find comfort in being alone and separate and untouchable. I would find safety in my own little world. No one could hurt me there. I could escape! Because Mom was caught up in the circumstances of Uncle Colin's tirade, there were no loving arms for me to run to. Mom was a victim too. Together, with no loving arms, there were no words of love or support. There was nothing but the island I made myself into; impregnable and alone, and sheltered from harm. No one could hurt me there. The thing was that the island was where I still retreated as an adult. Many times, when I was suddenly going quiet, or into depression, was a time of retreating to my safe island, to be alone. People could be all around me, but I was alone. All alone and no one could hurt me. What caused me to do it I never knew, but it was instant and totally out of nowhere, and the pain I tried to avoid had become a part of me.

While there were other things to look at within, these were the two main areas to focus on. In reality, when the thoughts came that put the false blame on me, I had to process that thought afresh in my thinking and put the blame where it belonged. And when I sensed myself retreating to my island, I needed to take control and choose not to retreat, but rather to just simply tell myself I am not going there. Such simple techniques worked really well once I had begun to recognize the process that needed to be stopped.

I saw the psychologist for around six visits, and my life was turned around in that short amount of time. Each week, I did my homework, and together with the lord came breakthroughs little by little. At the end of our time together, the lady told me she had never worked with anyone with so much personal insight about themselves. Funny, isn't it, that with all my insight, I at first could not recognize the problems, or see the solutions that she pointed me to.

As unbelievable as it seems, after just a few visits I was pain free. Years and years of inner pain just seemed to evaporate away. There was an almost funny side to this, too. I had, for as long as I could remember, always told myself that if things got too bad, I could always kill myself. It was a bit of a throwaway line, but it was a sort of coping mechanism for me, and something I really believed. Eventually, in my pain free days, life threw up a situation that was hard to face and deal with. My mind went immediately to the thought, "No worries, if it gets too bad, I can always kill myself", but the funny thing was, that as soon as that thought entered my mind, a new thought countered with, "that is not an option anymore." The great thing was, emotionally, I really did know it was not an option anymore. It now seemed like such a weird statement, that was totally foreign to the person I had now become.

And, there was an added bonus for me. For the first time, a new thing happened, I was genuinely happy to celebrate my birthday. This was something I had never done. I didn't even allow my wife to buy me a birthday present or celebrate my birthday in any way. It was all a part of believing that I should never have been born. Now, finally I could accept that it was all right for me to have been born, and that any issues other people had with that was their problem.

It is now fourteen years since my depression left. Yes, I'm a normal person and can have my days of feeling a bit down about life's circumstances, but there is none of the pain I used to experience. The pain has gone. The truly debilitating pain has gone. Hallelujah!

It may seem unbelievable to say what I am about to say, but after travelling with the deep depression and pain for so many years and then experiencing being set free from it, I now have a strange overwhelming experience in my day-to-day life. It truly feels somewhat weird but life now seems so easy to live.

Chapter 18

Nothing to Everything

As an illegitimate child in the era I grew up in, I had nothing legally. I did not have a legally recognized father. I did not have my father's name. I had no inheritance. I had no financial support from my father. I had no official family on my father's side. I lost grandparents, uncles and aunts, cousins, etc. I was seen as an outcast of society, to be avoided.

My identity was bound up in a derogatory term, that was even used as a swear word. And amazingly, none of this was my fault. It just so happened, that before I was even conceived, other people made decisions, the consequences of which I would have to live every day of my life with.

On reflection, I had nothing.

But then I was born again.

"Jesus replied, 'Very truly I tell you, no one can see the kingdom of God unless they are born again.'" (John 3:3 NIV)

I became a child of God by adoption.

"The Spirit you received does not make you slaves, so that you live in fear again; rather, the Spirit you received brought about your adoption to sonship. And by him we cry, "Abba, Father." (Romans 8:15 NIV)

This gave me legal rights in God's Kingdom. I now had a heavenly father. I am a brother of him whose name is above all names. I have received the Holy Spirit as a confirmation of God's love and eternal acceptance. I have an eternal inheritance, abundantly above anything this world can offer. I have a father who provides my daily bread, and provides all the essentials I need. I have been born into the family of God, and have relatives beyond measure. I have words to describe my position now that are positive and life giving. Before I was even conceived, God decided in eternity past, that all his abundant variations of wealth are available to me, through his one and only son. I can live every day with the consequences of God's grace in my life.

I grew up thinking I had nothing, and now I see I have gone from having nothing, to having everything I could ever need or desire, in and through Christ Jesus. I now see through a glass darkly but in the fullness of time all will be revealed and nothing shall be hid. From nothing to everything, not bad is it? And, the amazing thing is, I could never have raised enough money to purchase it. There was no way I could have done any good deeds or actions of any sort to earn it. It all came in full measure, by the grace of God, in that briefest of moments in time, "in the twinkling of an eye." Thank you, Jesus. Thank you, Holy Spirit. Thank you, heavenly father. I am looking forward to that first hug in heaven.

And now, I look forward to the great day of ultimate transformation and fulfillment.

"In a flash, in the twinkling of an eye, at the last trumpet. For the trumpet will sound, the dead will be raised imperishable, and we will be changed." (I Cor. 15:52 NIV)

"Maranatha!"

www.ingramcontent.com/pod-product-compliance
Lightning Source LLC
Chambersburg PA
CBHW070501090426
42735CB00012B/2649